ESP32 MicroPython Programn
Essential Guide for Absolute Beginners & IoT
Projects

First Edition
Sarful Hassan

Preface

ESP32 MicroPython Programming: An Essential Guide for Absolute Beginners & IoT Projects is designed to provide a hands-on, project-oriented approach for learning how to program the ESP32 microcontroller using MicroPython. This book is written for those who are new to both the ESP32 and MicroPython, as well as experienced developers who want to dive into IoT projects. Whether you are an absolute beginner or have some programming background, this guide will take you through each step, from setting up the tools to building real-world applications.

Who This Book Is For

This book is for:

- Absolute beginners with little to no programming experience.
- Hobbyists and makers who are interested in creating IoT projects.
- Developers and engineers who want to quickly get started with MicroPython on ESP32.
- Students and educators looking for a practical, project-based guide to embedded systems.

How This Book Is Organized

This book is organized into three parts:

1. **Part 1: Introduction to ESP32 and MicroPython** – Guides you through setting up the ESP32 and introduces the basics of MicroPython programming.
2. **Part 2: Programming Fundamentals with MicroPython** – Explores core programming concepts such as variables, data types, functions, GPIO operations, and control structures, using practical examples.
3. **Part 3: Get Started with IoT Using MicroPython** – Focuses on building IoT applications by leveraging Wi-Fi, creating web servers, and integrating sensors and actuators into your projects.

Each part contains chapters that build upon one another to create a complete learning path from beginner to intermediate-level IoT developer.

What Was Left Out

To keep this book focused on essential skills, advanced topics such as deep learning on microcontrollers, extensive error handling, and advanced hardware debugging techniques were omitted. Additionally, while we touch on many IoT concepts, topics like cloud integration and long-range communication (LoRa) are left out, as they require more specialized hardware and deeper knowledge.

Code Style (About the Code)

The code examples in this book are written in a clear, beginner-friendly style, following standard MicroPython conventions. Code is formatted with consistent indentation, meaningful variable names, and simple comments to explain each step. You will find code snippets throughout the book to demonstrate each concept, and complete projects are provided for you to follow along.

MicroPython Platform Release Notes

This book is based on MicroPython Version 1.15 or later. As MicroPython is an open-source project with frequent updates, you may find minor differences between the book's examples and newer versions. It is recommended to visit the official MicroPython documentation for any updates that might affect your code.

Notes on the First Edition

This is the first edition of **ESP32 MicroPython Programming: An Essential Guide for Absolute Beginners & IoT Projects**. As the field of IoT and embedded systems is evolving rapidly, we encourage readers to send feedback, corrections, and suggestions for future editions.

Conventions Used in This Book

The following conventions are used throughout the book:

- **Code blocks**: Represented in monospace font to differentiate from regular text.
- **Commands**: Shown as you would type them into a terminal or MicroPython REPL.
- **Warnings and tips**: Special notes are highlighted to help you avoid common mistakes.

Using Code Examples

All the code examples provided in this book are free to use and modify in your own projects. We encourage you to experiment with the code to reinforce your understanding of MicroPython and ESP32 programming.

MechatronicsLAB Online Learning

For additional resources, tutorials, and online courses, visit **MechatronicsLAB** at mechatronicslab.net. You can find supplementary materials for this book, as well as additional projects and guides.

For inquiries, feel free to contact us at **mechatronicslab@gmail.com**.

How to Contact Us

We welcome your feedback. You can reach us via:

- Email: **mechatronicslab@gmail.com**
- Website: mechatronicslab.net

Acknowledgments for the First Edition

I would like to extend my deepest thanks to the entire MechatronicsLAB team, my family, and all those who helped make this book possible. Special thanks to the developers of MicroPython and the open-source community for providing the tools and inspiration to create this guide.

Copyright

Disclaimer

Table of Contents

Part 1: Introduction to ESP32 and ESP8266 and MicroPython

Chapter-1 Introduction of ESP32 and ESP8266

The **ESP32** and **ESP8266** are microcontrollers developed by **Espressif Systems**, commonly used in **Internet of Things (IoT)** projects. These microcontrollers are known for their **built-in Wi-Fi** capabilities, which make them highly popular for connecting devices to the internet and creating smart, connected systems. Both are affordable and widely used, but they have different levels of power, features, and applications, making them suitable for different use cases.

- **ESP32**: Designed to be a high-performance microcontroller with dual-core processing, Wi-Fi, and Bluetooth capabilities, the ESP32 is ideal for more advanced IoT projects. It is suitable for applications where more computing power, additional features, and enhanced connectivity are needed.
- **ESP8266**: Known for its low cost and built-in Wi-Fi, the ESP8266 is ideal for simpler IoT projects, particularly for beginners or budget-conscious makers. It's capable of handling basic tasks and is perfect for projects that do not require the higher performance or additional connectivity options found in the ESP32.

Introduction to ESP32

The **ESP32** is a powerful and versatile microcontroller unit (MCU) created by Espressif Systems, specifically designed to enable connected, smart, and interactive devices. The key highlights of the ESP32 are:

- **Dual-Core Processor**: The ESP32 features two Xtensa LX6 processors, each capable of running up to **240 MHz**. This dual-core setup makes it powerful enough for multitasking and managing different operations simultaneously, which is beneficial in many IoT scenarios.

- **Connectivity**: It supports **Wi-Fi** (802.11 b/g/n) and **Bluetooth**, including **Bluetooth Low Energy (BLE)**. This makes the ESP32 versatile, as it can connect to the internet or other devices via Bluetooth.
- **Power Management**: The ESP32 is known for its various **low-power modes**, which makes it ideal for battery-powered applications. It can operate in **deep sleep mode** with very low power consumption, which is an essential feature for IoT projects that need to last long on a single battery charge.
- **Peripherals and GPIO**: The ESP32 comes with a wide range of **GPIO (General Purpose Input/Output) pins**, which can be used to connect sensors, LEDs, buttons, and other devices. It also has built-in modules like **analog-to-digital converters (ADC)**, **touch sensors**, and a **temperature sensor**.
- **Applications**: It is well-suited for **smart home automation**, **wearables**, **wireless sensors**, and **other advanced IoT projects** that require a high level of connectivity and computation power.

Introduction to ESP8266

The **ESP8266** is an earlier microcontroller model from Espressif Systems, widely popular for its affordability and integrated Wi-Fi. Key characteristics of the ESP8266 are:

- **Single-Core Processor**: The ESP8266 features a **32-bit Tensilica L106 processor**, running at speeds between **80 MHz and 160 MHz**. While it's not as powerful as the ESP32, it is sufficient for less demanding IoT projects, especially those that don't require extensive data processing.
- **Built-in Wi-Fi**: The ESP8266 has a built-in **Wi-Fi module**, making it perfect for connecting small devices to the internet without needing an external Wi-Fi chip. It supports standard Wi-Fi protocols for internet access.
- **Cost-Effectiveness**: The ESP8266 is known for being **highly affordable**, which is why it became popular with hobbyists and makers. It provides a low-cost way to add Wi-Fi capabilities to electronics.

- **GPIO and Connectivity**: It has a limited number of **GPIO pins** compared to the ESP32, which limits the number of sensors and peripherals that can be connected simultaneously. Nevertheless, it supports common communication protocols like **SPI, I2C**, and **UART**, making it versatile enough for many smaller projects.
- **Applications**: The ESP8266 is ideal for simple projects such as **smart light switches**, **basic wireless sensors**, and **simple automation devices** where a low-cost solution is needed.

Comparison between ESP32 and ESP8266

To help understand the differences and choose between ESP32 and ESP8266, let's compare their features:

1. **Processing Power**:
   - **ESP32**: Features a **dual-core processor**, running up to **240 MHz**, providing more processing power for demanding applications.
   - **ESP8266**: Has a **single-core processor** running at **80-160 MHz**, sufficient for simple tasks and straightforward IoT projects.
2. **Connectivity**:
   - **ESP32**: Offers both **Wi-Fi** and **Bluetooth (including BLE)** connectivity. This dual connectivity makes it ideal for projects that require a variety of communication options.
   - **ESP8266**: Offers only **Wi-Fi** connectivity, making it great for basic IoT projects that involve internet communication without the need for Bluetooth.
3. **Power Consumption**:
   - **ESP32**: Comes with advanced power-saving features, including multiple power modes (like **deep sleep mode**), which make it suitable for battery-operated projects.
   - **ESP8266**: Also supports power-saving, but it is less efficient than the ESP32, which may affect long-term battery life in some projects.

4. **GPIO and Peripherals**:
    - **ESP32**: Has more **GPIO pins** and a richer set of built-in peripherals, including touch sensors, analog inputs, and a temperature sensor, giving more flexibility for complex projects.
    - **ESP8266**: Has fewer GPIO pins, limiting the number of devices that can be connected, but is still capable of handling basic hardware interfaces and common sensors.
5. **Price**:
    - **ESP8266**: **Cheaper** compared to the ESP32, making it the preferred option for budget projects and for beginners just getting into IoT.
    - **ESP32**: Slightly **more expensive** but worth the cost for projects that require more features and better performance.
6. **Suitability for Projects**:
    - **ESP32**: Best for **advanced IoT projects**, requiring high processing power, Bluetooth connectivity, and multiple sensor inputs. Examples include **smart home automation systems**, **wearable devices**, and **complex sensors**.
    - **ESP8266**: Great for **entry-level and basic IoT projects**, where cost and simplicity are the main factors. It is perfect for **home automation**, such as smart lights and switches, where only Wi-Fi is required.

History and Evolution of ESP8266 and ESP32

Release Timeline

The ESP8266 and ESP32 microcontrollers have significantly impacted the development of IoT solutions by providing affordable and powerful connectivity options. Here's a look at their release history:

- **ESP8266 Release Timeline**:
    - **2014**: The **ESP8266** was first introduced by Espressif Systems, becoming a game changer due to its integrated Wi-Fi capabilities at a very low cost. It

initially gained popularity with hobbyists and DIY makers.

- o **Late 2014 - 2015**: The ESP8266 gained widespread adoption thanks to the open availability of software development tools (SDKs) that allowed developers to easily create custom firmware.
- **ESP32 Release Timeline**:
  - o **2016**: Espressif Systems launched the **ESP32**, which was developed as a more powerful successor to the ESP8266. It included enhanced features like dual-core processing, Bluetooth connectivity, and improved power efficiency.
  - o **Late 2016 - 2017**: The ESP32 quickly caught the attention of developers and IoT enthusiasts, largely due to its increased processing power and additional features.

Timeline of Hardware Updates and Firmware Improvements

ESP8266 Hardware and Firmware Evolution:

- **2014**: The initial version of ESP8266 had limited software support and was primarily used in basic Wi-Fi-enabled projects.
- **2015 - 2016**: Espressif improved SDK support, adding more stable and feature-rich firmware. This enabled developers to take advantage of better Wi-Fi stability, power management, and the ability to customize applications.
- **NodeMCU Boards**: Popular third-party development boards, like NodeMCU, made ESP8266 more accessible by adding USB connectivity, voltage regulators, and breakout pins.

ESP32 Hardware and Firmware Evolution:

- **2016**: The first ESP32 modules, like the ESP-WROOM-32, were released. They included new features such as Bluetooth Low Energy (BLE) and multiple analog and digital peripherals.
- **2017 - 2018**: Firmware updates focused on improving Bluetooth stack performance, reducing power consumption, and optimizing GPIO and I/O functions.

- **New Variants**: Different versions of the ESP32 module have been introduced to cater to specific needs, such as the **ESP32-S2** (targeted towards security-sensitive applications) and **ESP32-C3** (based on the RISC-V architecture for cost-effective solutions).

ESP8266 to ESP32: The Evolution
Reasons for the Development of ESP32

The **ESP8266** was revolutionary for making Wi-Fi connectivity affordable, but it had some limitations, which led to the development of the **ESP32**. Key reasons for this evolution include:

- **Enhanced Processing Power**: The ESP8266 has a single-core processor with limited power, which restricts its multitasking capabilities. The ESP32 was developed with **dual-core processors** to provide more power for handling multiple tasks efficiently.
- **Additional Connectivity Options**: While the ESP8266 only supported Wi-Fi, the ESP32 introduced **Bluetooth** and **Bluetooth Low Energy (BLE)** capabilities, enabling a wider range of connectivity options.
- **Power Efficiency**: One key drawback of the ESP8266 was its relatively high power consumption for battery-operated applications. The ESP32 offers **low-power modes** and better power management, making it suitable for portable devices.

Enhancements Over ESP8266
The **ESP32** includes several significant improvements over the **ESP8266**:

- **More GPIO Pins**: The ESP32 features more GPIO pins, which provides greater flexibility in connecting peripherals, sensors, and other hardware.
- **Dual-Core Processor**: Unlike the single-core ESP8266, the ESP32 features a **dual-core Xtensa LX6 processor**, which enables better multitasking and overall performance.

- **Built-in Peripherals**: The ESP32 comes with a host of built-in peripherals, such as **analog-to-digital converters (ADCs)**, **capacitive touch sensors**, **temperature sensors**, and even **digital-to-analog converters (DACs)**.
- **Multiple Communication Interfaces**: The ESP32 supports **SPI**, **I2C**, **UART**, and **CAN**, allowing for more versatile communication between components.

Impact on IoT Community

How ESP8266 Revolutionised Affordable Wi-Fi Modules

The **ESP8266** marked a revolutionary shift in the IoT community by significantly reducing the cost of adding Wi-Fi capabilities to electronic devices. Before the ESP8266, Wi-Fi modules were often costly, making it impractical for smaller projects or DIY enthusiasts. Key impacts of the ESP8266 include:

- **Lowered Barriers to Entry**: The low cost and ease of use of the ESP8266 democratized access to Wi-Fi-enabled microcontrollers, making them accessible for hobbyists, students, and developers on a budget.
- **Community and Ecosystem Growth**: The availability of open-source SDKs and extensive community support helped foster a large and engaged developer base. This resulted in the rapid growth of tutorials, libraries, and projects that further popularized the module.
- **Rise of DIY IoT Projects**: ESP8266 enabled the development of countless **DIY projects**, such as smart lights, Wi-Fi weather stations, and connected sensors, inspiring more people to engage in IoT development.

The Adoption of ESP32 in Advanced IoT Applications

The **ESP32** took the success of the ESP8266 a step further by introducing features that made it suitable for more advanced IoT applications:

- **Complex Applications**: With its **dual-core processing**, **Bluetooth**, and more GPIO options, the ESP32 is commonly used in complex projects such as **robotics**, **real-time monitoring systems**, and **wearables**.

- **Industrial IoT**: The increased power and versatility of the ESP32 have also made it a popular choice in industrial IoT (IIoT) applications, such as remote monitoring, data logging, and automation systems.
- **Expanded Use Cases**: Bluetooth and Bluetooth Low Energy (BLE) support have allowed the ESP32 to be used in projects that require device-to-device communication, such as **smart health** devices, **home automation**, and **mesh networks**.

Future of ESP32 and ESP8266 in IoT

Future of ESP8266

- **Continued Use in Basic IoT Projects**: Given its affordability, the **ESP8266** is likely to remain a popular choice for basic IoT projects that do not require high processing power or Bluetooth. It will continue to be used by beginners and makers looking to create simple, internet-connected devices.
- **Educational Use**: The ESP8266 will remain an educational tool for learning about IoT and microcontrollers. Its simplicity makes it an ideal choice for introducing students and new developers to Wi-Fi-based projects.

Future of ESP32

- **Expanded Industrial Applications**: With its robust processing capabilities and connectivity options, the **ESP32** will continue to be adopted in more advanced industrial applications and environments where more reliable and flexible connectivity is needed.
- **Growing Integration with AI and Machine Learning**: As AI and edge computing become more prevalent, the ESP32, with its processing power, is well-positioned to support **machine learning models** at the edge, making it suitable for applications like **smart cameras**, **voice recognition**, and **predictive maintenance**.
- **New Variants and Features**: Espressif has continued to expand the ESP32 family with variants like **ESP32-S3** and **ESP32-C3**, each with unique features that cater to specific use cases (e.g., enhanced AI capabilities, reduced cost).

This diversification ensures that the ESP32 line remains adaptable and versatile for various IoT needs.

Pinout and Hardware Layout

Understanding the pinout and hardware layout of microcontrollers like **ESP32** and **ESP8266** is essential for connecting sensors, peripherals, and other electronic components effectively. Both ESP32 and ESP8266 have different sets of pins with specific functions that define their use cases in projects.

ESP32 Pinout Diagram

The **ESP32** microcontroller comes with numerous **GPIO pins** and a variety of other specialized pins that can be used for different purposes. Here's a high-level description of the **ESP32 pinout**:

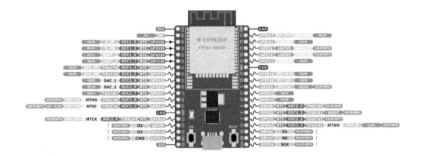

- **GPIO Pins**: The ESP32 typically has **36 GPIO pins** (depending on the variant). These pins can be used as digital inputs or outputs. Many of these pins also have additional functions, such as PWM, ADC, or touch sensors.
- **Power Pins**:
    - **3.3V Pin**: Supplies 3.3 volts of power to the board.
    - **Vin Pin**: This pin is used to power the ESP32 from an external 5V power source.
    - **Ground (GND) Pins**: Connect to the ground of the circuit.
- **Analog Input Pins (ADC)**: The ESP32 has multiple ADC pins that can be used to read analog sensors. There are **18 channels** available, with a resolution of up to **12 bits**.

- **Touch Sensors**: The ESP32 has **capacitive touch pins** (T0 to T9), allowing for touch-based input detection.
- **UART, SPI, I2C, and PWM Pins**: These pins provide communication interfaces to connect peripherals.
  - **UART**: Supports up to 3 UART interfaces for serial communication.
  - **SPI/I2C**: Multiple SPI and I2C pins allow for interfacing with sensors and other devices.
  - **PWM**: Most GPIOs can be used for **PWM** (Pulse Width Modulation), useful for controlling LEDs and motors.
- **Other Special Pins**:
  - **EN Pin**: The **Enable** pin (EN) is used to reset the microcontroller.
  - **Boot Pin (IO0)**: Used to put the ESP32 into **bootloader mode** for uploading firmware.

ESP8266 Pinout Diagram

The **ESP8266** has fewer pins compared to the ESP32, and understanding its pinout is crucial for using it effectively in simpler projects.

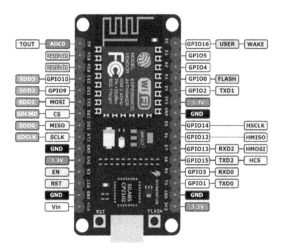

- **GPIO Pins**: The ESP8266 generally has **17 GPIO pins** available (depending on the development board). These pins serve multiple functions and can be configured as digital input or output.

- **Power Pins**:
  - **3.3V Pin**: Supplies power to the ESP8266 (typically operates at 3.3V).
  - **Vin Pin**: Powers the module with an input voltage range of 4.5V to 12V, depending on the board.
  - **Ground (GND) Pins**: Connects to the ground of the circuit.
- **Analog Input Pin (ADC0)**: The ESP8266 has **one analog input pin** (ADC0), which can measure voltages from 0 to 1V.
- **UART, SPI, I2C, and PWM Pins**:
  - **UART**: Supports serial communication for programming and debugging.
  - **SPI/I2C**: Fewer communication options compared to ESP32, but SPI and I2C are still supported for external components.
  - **PWM**: Limited GPIO pins can be configured for PWM, mainly for controlling simple components like LEDs.
- **CH_PD Pin**: The **Chip Power-Down** pin is used to enable or disable the chip.

Pin Functions and Description
Power Pins
- **ESP32 and ESP8266 both have 3.3V and GND pins** for power supply. It's crucial to ensure that the **input voltage** is regulated to prevent damaging the microcontrollers.
- The **Vin pin** can be used to provide external power; however, the voltage requirements for ESP32 and ESP8266 may vary slightly depending on the board.

Input/Output Pins
- Both **ESP32** and **ESP8266** GPIO pins can be configured as **inputs or outputs**, making them versatile for controlling components like LEDs, motors, or reading sensor values.
- **ESP32**: Offers **more GPIO pins** (typically 36), which allows more components to be connected simultaneously.

- **ESP8266**: Offers fewer GPIO pins (usually **17**), which can be a limitation when attempting to connect multiple peripherals.

GPIO Limitations and Considerations

- **ESP32**:
  - Not all GPIO pins are available for general use. Some pins have specific functions (e.g., flash, boot mode) and should be avoided in general-purpose use unless configured correctly.
  - Pins like **GPIO6 to GPIO11** are used for the internal flash and should **not** be used for other purposes.
- **ESP8266**:
  - **GPIO0, GPIO2, and GPIO15**: These pins have special functions during boot mode and should be used carefully to avoid conflicts during power-up.
  - **Limited Number of GPIOs**: With fewer GPIOs, you may need to use **multiplexing** techniques or **GPIO expanders** to connect additional components.

Interrupt Capabilities

- **ESP32**: Supports **interrupts** on almost all GPIO pins. This feature is crucial when you need the microcontroller to respond immediately to an event, like a button press.
- **ESP8266**: Interrupts are also supported but are more limited. Care should be taken to avoid using certain pins that may not properly support interrupts.

Analog Input Limitations

- **ESP32**:
  - The ESP32 has **multiple ADC channels** (up to 18), with a 12-bit resolution, which provides more precise analog readings.
  - However, the **ADC** is known to be **non-linear**, and calibration may be required to get accurate results.
- **ESP8266**:
  - The **ESP8266** has only **one ADC pin** (ADC0), and its range is limited to 0-1V, which can be restrictive when trying to read analog signals with higher voltages.

- A voltage divider may be needed to bring the input voltage within the acceptable range of the ADC.

GPIO Pin Details and Usage for ESP32 and ESP8266

GPIO Pin Number	Pin Type	ESP 32	ESP8 266	Use
GPIO 0	Digital I/O	Yes	Yes	Boot mode selection, LED control
GPIO 1 (TX)	UART TX	Yes	Yes	Serial communication (data transmission)
GPIO 2	Digital I/O	Yes	Yes	LED control, status indication
GPIO 3 (RX)	UART RX	Yes	Yes	Serial communication (data reception)
GPIO 4	Digital I/O	Yes	Yes	General-purpose tasks, sensors, LEDs
GPIO 5	Digital I/O	Yes	Yes	Motor control, PWM
GPIO 6-11	Flash Memory	No	No	Reserved (do not use)
GPIO 12	Digital I/O	Yes	Yes	General-purpose tasks, output devices
GPIO 13	Digital I/O, PWM	Yes	Yes	LED dimming, motor control

GPIO 14	Digital I/O, PWM	Yes	Yes	PWM for motor or LED, sensor input
GPIO 15	Digital I/O, PWM	Yes	Yes	PWM, sensor or device control
GPIO 16	Digital I/O, Wake	Yes	Yes	Wake from deep sleep, low-power projects
GPIO 17	Digital I/O	Yes	No	General-purpose tasks
GPIO 18	SPI SCK	Yes	No	SPI communication (clock line)
GPIO 19	SPI MISO	Yes	No	SPI communication (data reception)
GPIO 21	I2C SDA	Yes	No	I2C communication (data line)
GPIO 22	I2C SCL	Yes	No	I2C communication (clock line)
GPIO 23	SPI MOSI	Yes	No	SPI communication (data transmission)
GPIO 25-27	Digital I/O, ADC	Yes	No	Reading analog values from sensors
GPIO 32-39	ADC	Yes	No	Analog input (e.g., sensors like LDRs)

Power Supply Requirements:

Voltage Range and Power Consumption:

- **ESP32**: The ESP32 operates within a voltage range of **3.0V to 3.6V**, with an ideal input voltage of **3.3V**. It is capable of drawing a substantial amount of current, especially during Wi-Fi transmission. During peak usage (like Wi-Fi transmission), the ESP32 can consume around **160-240 mA**, while in idle mode, it typically consumes around **20-30 mA**.
- **ESP8266**: The ESP8266 also operates in a voltage range of **3.0V to 3.6V**, typically running at **3.3V**. Its power consumption is slightly lower than that of the ESP32, with peak currents reaching **170 mA** during Wi-Fi transmission. In idle mode, the current draw is roughly **10-20 mA**.

Power Management Hardware: Both ESP32 and ESP8266 have built-in capabilities to manage power consumption effectively:

- **Voltage Regulators**: Most development boards for the ESP32 and ESP8266 (such as NodeMCU or ESP32 DevKit) come with onboard **voltage regulators** that convert higher input voltages (like 5V from USB) to the required **3.3V** for the microcontroller. These voltage regulators ensure that the input power is within the safe operating range.
- **Decoupling Capacitors**: To ensure stable voltage supply and avoid fluctuations during peak power usage, decoupling capacitors are often included on development boards.

Battery Power and USB Power Options:

- **Battery Power**: Both ESP32 and ESP8266 can be powered using batteries, making them ideal for portable projects. Typical battery options include **Li-ion/Li-Po** batteries (3.7V nominal voltage). For battery-powered setups, a voltage regulator is necessary to step down the voltage to **3.3V**. The ESP32 is designed with several power-saving modes, making it suitable for long-term battery-powered applications.

- **USB Power**: Development boards for both ESP32 and ESP8266 generally have a **micro USB port** for powering and programming the microcontroller. The USB power supplies **5V**, which is then regulated down to **3.3V** on the board.

Current Draw During Different States:
Active Mode:
- **ESP32**: In active mode, when all components are running, including Wi-Fi, the ESP32 can consume between **160-240 mA**. This high power draw occurs primarily during transmission and data processing. The dual-core processor adds to the power requirements when both cores are in operation.
- **ESP8266**: In active mode with Wi-Fi enabled, the ESP8266 draws about **150-170 mA**. This is slightly lower compared to the ESP32 due to its simpler architecture and lower processing power.

Sleep Mode:
- **ESP32**: The ESP32 is highly optimized for low-power operation, offering several sleep modes, including **light sleep** and **deep sleep**. In **deep sleep mode**, the ESP32 can reduce its power consumption to around **10 µA**, making it suitable for battery-powered devices where long operational life is required. **Light sleep** typically uses a bit more power, around **1-5 mA**.
- **ESP8266**: The ESP8266 also offers sleep modes, although they are less sophisticated compared to the ESP32. In **deep sleep mode**, the ESP8266 can reduce power consumption to about **20 µA**, which is higher than the ESP32. The wake-up process from deep sleep is relatively slower, which may affect its use in some applications requiring quick responses.

Development Environment and Getting Started

Programming Platforms:

MicroPython: **MicroPython** is a popular option for those who prefer scripting over compiled code. It is ideal for rapid prototyping, and both the **ESP32** and **ESP8266** support MicroPython.

- MicroPython can be flashed onto the device, allowing you to write Python scripts to interact with the hardware. It's a great option for beginners who already have some familiarity with Python programming.
- Tools like **Thonny** or **uPyCraft** IDEs make it easy to connect to and program MicroPython on ESP modules.

Required Hardware and Tools:

USB-to-Serial Converter: Most **ESP32** and **ESP8266** development boards, like NodeMCU and ESP32 DevKit, come with a built-in USB-to-serial converter, allowing easy connection to your computer via USB. For standalone modules (e.g., ESP-12 or ESP-01), an external **USB-to-Serial converter** (e.g., **CP2102** or **FTDI232**) is required for flashing and communication.

Power Supply Modules: For reliable operation, a **power supply module** is often needed to provide a stable **3.3V** supply. This can be achieved via:
- **USB Power**: The development boards can be powered through a USB cable.
- **Battery Power**: **Li-ion/Li-Po** batteries are commonly used, especially for portable projects.

Basic Troubleshooting for Setup (Driver Issues, Flashing Problems):

Driver Issues:
- If your computer does not recognize the ESP32 or ESP8266, you may need to install drivers for **USB-to-Serial chips** like **CP2102**, **CH340**, or **FTDI**.
- Ensure that the correct COM port is selected in the **Arduino IDE** under **Tools > Port**.

Flashing Problems:
- **Common Errors**: "Failed to connect to ESP32" is a common error when the microcontroller is not in bootloader mode. Press and hold the **BOOT** button while uploading code to put the ESP32 in flashing mode.
- Ensure the **baud rate** is set correctly (usually *115200*).

Flashing Firmware:
Using ESP-Tool to Flash:
- **ESP-Tool** is a command-line utility provided by Espressif for flashing firmware onto ESP32 and ESP8266 devices.
- **Installation**: Install `esptool` using Python's package manager: *pip install esptool*
- **Usage**: Connect your ESP board and run the following command to erase the flash memory: *esptool.py erase_flash* To flash new firmware: *esptool.py --port COM3 write_flash -z 0x0000 firmware.bin* Replace *COM3* with the appropriate port (e.g., */dev/ttyUSB0* on Linux) and *firmware.bin* with the path to your firmware file.

Troubleshooting Common Issues:
USB Connectivity Problems (Beyond Initial Setup): Even after setting up the initial development environment, you might encounter USB connectivity issues:
- **USB Port Not Recognized**:
  - *Check USB Cable*: Some USB cables are power-only and do not support data transfer. Make sure you are using a **data-capable USB cable**.
  - *Port Selection*: Ensure the correct **COM port** is selected in the **Arduino IDE** under **Tools > Port**.
  - *Reinstall Drivers*: Sometimes, drivers may become corrupted. Reinstalling drivers for **CP2102**, **CH340**, or **FTDI** can help resolve recognition issues.
- **Board Keeps Disconnecting**:
  - *Power Supply Issue*: Ensure that the board is receiving stable power. A poor-quality USB cable or insufficient power from the USB port can cause

disconnections. Using a powered USB hub can provide a more stable power supply.

- o *USB Port Overload*: Avoid plugging multiple power-consuming devices into the same USB hub as your ESP board, as this may cause voltage drops, resulting in random disconnections.

Wi-Fi Connectivity Issues:
- **Unable to Connect to Wi-Fi**:
  - o *Wrong Credentials*: Double-check the **SSID** and **password**. Simple typos can lead to connection failures.
  - o *Wi-Fi Signal Strength*: Place the ESP module closer to the router or access point, and ensure there aren't many obstacles. Use the **WiFi.RSSI()** function in **Arduino IDE** or similar methods to check signal strength.
  - o *Channel Overcrowding*: Many Wi-Fi networks on the same channel can cause interference. If possible, change the router's channel to a less crowded one.
- **Intermittent Wi-Fi Disconnection**:
  - o *Power Supply Stability*: Ensure a stable power supply, as Wi-Fi transmission draws significant current. Voltage fluctuations can cause the microcontroller to reset or disconnect from Wi-Fi.
  - o *Firmware Update*: Older firmware may have issues maintaining a stable Wi-Fi connection. Updating to the latest **ESP32** or **ESP8266 firmware** can resolve such issues.

Debugging Tools and Techniques:
- **Serial Monitor**:
  - o The **Serial Monitor** in **Arduino IDE** is a fundamental tool for debugging. Use *Serial.print()* statements to understand the flow of your code and identify where errors occur.

- **Logic Analyzers**:
  - For communication issues (such as **I2C** or **SPI**), a **logic analyzer** can help you understand what data is being transmitted and identify where errors might be occurring.
- **ESP-IDF Monitor**:
  - If using **ESP-IDF**, the integrated **ESP-IDF Monitor** provides useful logs and real-time debugging information. It is especially useful for understanding deeper issues like crashes or stack traces.

Best Practices for Using ESP32/ESP8266:

Power Supply Stability:
- Ensure a **reliable 3.3V power supply**. Both ESP32 and ESP8266 can draw spikes of current during Wi-Fi transmissions. If you are using a linear regulator, make sure it can handle at least **500 mA** of current.
- When using battery power, consider a **Li-Po battery** with a **DC-DC buck converter** to ensure stable voltage, as voltage drops can cause unexpected reboots.

Proper GPIO Usage:
- **ESP32**: Not all GPIO pins are available for general use, as some are used internally by the microcontroller (e.g., for flash or boot). Avoid using **GPIO6 to GPIO11** for other purposes, as these are connected to the integrated flash memory.
- **ESP8266**: Special GPIO pins like **GPIO0**, **GPIO2**, and **GPIO15** are involved in the boot process. Ensure proper connections if these pins are used, as incorrect connections can cause the board to not boot correctly.
- Use **current-limiting resistors** (typically **220 ohms to 1k ohms**) when connecting LEDs or other components to GPIO pins to protect both the pins and external components.

Antenna Placement for Wi-Fi:

- **Avoid Obstacles**: The onboard antenna should not be obstructed by metal components, power supplies, or other electronics that could interfere with signal transmission.
- **Distance from Power Sources**: Place the ESP module away from power supplies, as electromagnetic interference can degrade Wi-Fi performance.
- **Proper Orientation**: The onboard PCB antenna is directional. Make sure the module is oriented so that the antenna faces outward for optimal coverage.

Chapter-2 Introduction to MicroPython

What is MicroPython?

MicroPython is a lightweight implementation of the Python 3 programming language that is designed to run on microcontrollers. It allows you to write simple Python scripts to control hardware components like LEDs, sensors, motors, and more. With MicroPython, beginners can easily interact with electronics using a language they may already be familiar with—Python. It's a powerful yet beginner-friendly option for those who want to start programming microcontrollers without having to learn complex low-level programming languages like C or C++.

MicroPython runs on various hardware platforms, and one of the most popular options is the ESP32, a low-cost microcontroller with built-in Wi-Fi and Bluetooth capabilities. This makes MicroPython ideal for IoT (Internet of Things) projects and for developing smart devices.

Why Choose MicroPython for ESP32?

1. **Beginner-Friendly and Easy to Learn**
   - MicroPython uses Python, which is known for its readability and simplicity. This makes it an excellent choice for beginners who want to get started with programming microcontrollers without having to deal with complicated syntax.

2. **Interactive Development**
   - MicroPython provides an interactive *REPL (Read-Eval-Print Loop)* environment that allows you to enter commands and see their effect immediately. This feature is highly beneficial for beginners to learn through experimentation and rapid prototyping.

3. **Rich Library Support**
   - MicroPython comes with a wide range of libraries that simplify common tasks like controlling *GPIO pins*, reading sensor data, and establishing *Wi-Fi connections*. This eliminates the need to write low-level code, allowing beginners to focus on building projects.

4. **Versatility of ESP32**
    - The *ESP32* is a powerful microcontroller with built-in Wi-Fi and Bluetooth, making it ideal for projects that require wireless connectivity. When combined with MicroPython, it becomes an easy and efficient platform for IoT projects, home automation, and more.
5. **Extensive Community Support**
    - The combination of *ESP32* and MicroPython has a large community of developers and enthusiasts. There are numerous tutorials, forums, and online resources available, which makes it easier for beginners to get help and find solutions to problems.

Setting Up the Development Environment

To start programming your *ESP32* with MicroPython, you will need to set up the development environment, which includes flashing the MicroPython firmware onto your *ESP32* and installing the necessary tools. Here's a step-by-step guide:

1. **Components Required**
    - *ESP32 board*
    - *Micro USB cable* (to connect the *ESP32* to your computer)
    - *Computer with internet access*
2. **Installing Python on Your Computer**
    - Before you can set up MicroPython, ensure that *Python 3* is installed on your computer. You can download Python from https://www.python.org/downloads/.
    - Once installed, verify the installation by opening a command prompt or terminal and typing: *python --version* This should return the version number of Python installed.
3. **Installing esptool**
    - *esptool* is a Python-based command-line utility that helps you flash the MicroPython firmware onto the *ESP32*.
    - Install *esptool* using *pip* (Python package manager) by typing: *pip install esptool*

4. **Downloading the MicroPython Firmware**
   - Go to the official MicroPython website https://micropython.org/download/esp32/ and download the latest firmware for *ESP32*. The file will have a *.bin* extension.

5. **Flashing MicroPython Firmware onto ESP32**
   - Connect your *ESP32* to your computer using the USB cable.
   - Open a command prompt or terminal and erase the current firmware using the command: *esptool.py --chip esp32 erase_flash*
   - Flash the MicroPython firmware onto the *ESP32* by typing: *esptool.py --chip esp32 --port COM3 write_flash -z 0x1000 firmware.bin* Replace *COM3* with the appropriate port number on your computer and *firmware.bin* with the path to the downloaded firmware.

6. **Connecting to the ESP32 with a Serial Tool**
   - To interact with your *ESP32*, you will need a serial communication tool like *PuTTY* or *Tera Term*, or you can use the command-line tool *screen*.
   - Alternatively, you can use the *Thonny IDE*, a beginner-friendly Python editor that has built-in support for MicroPython.

7. **Using Thonny IDE**
   - Download and install *Thonny IDE* from https://thonny.org/.
   - Connect your *ESP32* to your computer and open *Thonny*.
   - In *Thonny*, go to *Tools -> Options -> Interpreter* and select "MicroPython (ESP32)" as the interpreter. Set the appropriate port to communicate with your *ESP32*.
   - Once connected, you can start typing commands directly in the Python shell and upload scripts to the *ESP32*.

Chapter-3 Preparing Your Tools

Step 1: Installing Python and MicroPython IDEs

To program your *ESP32* using MicroPython, you need to prepare your computer. We need to install **Python** and set up an **IDE** (a tool where you can write and run your code).

1. Install Python

Python is the language we use to write code for MicroPython. Follow these steps to install it:
1. **Download Python**
   - Go to the official Python website: https://www.python.org/downloads/.
   - Download and install **Python 3** for your computer. During installation, **check the box that says "Add Python to PATH"**. This will make it easier to run Python commands later.
2. **Verify Python Installation**
   - Open your **command prompt** (on Windows) or **terminal** (on Mac/Linux).
   - Type this command:
     python --version
   - You should see a version number (e.g., *Python 3.9.1*). If you see this, it means Python is installed successfully!

2. Install a MicroPython IDE

An **IDE** (Integrated Development Environment) helps you write and manage your code easily. We recommend using either:
- **Thonny IDE**: This is a beginner-friendly tool that supports MicroPython.
   - Go to https://thonny.org/, download, and install it.
- **Mu Editor** (Recommended for Beginners):
   - Go to https://codewith.mu/.
   - Download and install *Mu Editor*, which is very simple and perfect for working with *ESP32*.

Step 2: Choosing and Setting Up Mu Editor

Let's use *Mu Editor* to make writing and uploading code to *ESP32* simple and fun.

1. Download and Install Mu Editor
- Go to https://codewith.mu/ and download *Mu Editor*.
- Install it by following the on-screen instructions.

2. Set Up Mu Editor for ESP32
- **Open Mu Editor**
  - After installing *Mu Editor*, open it.
- **Select the Mode**
  - When Mu Editor opens for the first time, it will ask you to choose a mode.
  - Select **"ESP MicroPython"** mode. This mode is specifically for programming ESP32 boards.
- **Connect Your ESP32**
  - Use a *Micro USB cable* to connect your *ESP32* to your computer. Make sure the cable is for both power and data transfer.
- **Test Connection Using REPL**
  - In *Mu Editor*, click the **REPL** button.
  - The REPL (Read-Eval-Print Loop) lets you type commands and see results immediately. It's a great way to test code and interact with your *ESP32* live.

Step 3: Flashing MicroPython Firmware to ESP32

Before you start programming, you need to "flash" the *MicroPython* firmware onto your *ESP32*. This will allow the board to understand Python code.

1. Download MicroPython Firmware
- Go to https://micropython.org/download/esp32/.
- Download the latest firmware for *ESP32*—it will be a *.bin* file.

2. Install esptool
- *esptool* is a small program that helps us flash the firmware onto *ESP32*.
- To install it, open the command prompt/terminal and type:
  - *pip install esptool*

3. Erase Existing Firmware

- Before flashing the new firmware, erase the current firmware on your *ESP32* to prepare it:
    - Type the following command:
      esptool.py --chip esp32 erase_flash
    - Make sure your *ESP32* is connected to your computer. This command will clear all the data from your ESP32.

4. Flash the MicroPython Firmware

- Now, let's install the MicroPython firmware:
    - Type the following command:
      esptool.py --chip esp32 --port COM3 write_flash -z 0x1000 firmware.bin
    - Replace *COM3* with the correct port for your computer:
        - On Windows, check **Device Manager** for the correct COM port (e.g., COM3).
        - On Linux or Mac, it might be something like */dev/ttyUSB0*.
    - Replace *firmware.bin* with the path to the firmware file you downloaded.

5. Verify Installation

- Once you have flashed the firmware, open *Mu Editor* again and click **REPL**.
- You should see the MicroPython prompt (>>>), which means your *ESP32* is ready to run Python code!

Part 2: Programming Fundamentals with MicroPython

Chapter 4. Variables and Data Types

This chapter introduces **variables and data types** in MicroPython. You will learn what variables are, how to create them, and how to use different data types to store information, such as numbers, text, and lists, while programming your ESP32.

Syntax Table: Variables and Data Types

Topic	Syntax	Simple Example
Integer Variable	*variable_name = int(value)*	*temperature = int(25)*
Float Variable	*variable_name = float(value)*	*distance = float(15.75)*
Boolean Variable	*variable_name = bool(value)*	*is_light_on = bool(True)*
NoneType Variable	*variable_name = None*	*button_state = None*
String Variable	*variable_name = str(value)* or *variable_name = "text value"*	*message = "Hello, World!"*
List Variable	*variable_name = [value1, value2, ...]*	*temperatures = [23, 25, 21]*
Tuple Variable	*variable_name = (value1, value2, ...)*	*coordinates = (10, 20)*
Bytes Variable	*variable_name = bytes([value1, value2, ...])*	*data = bytes([10, 20, 30])*

Set Variable	variable_name = {value1, value2, ...}	unique_numbers = {1, 2, 3}
Dictionary Variable	variable_name = {key1: value1, key2: value2, ...}	person = {"name": "Alice", "age": 25}

Introduction to Variables in MicroPython

What Are Variables?

A **variable** is like a storage box in your program where you can keep different kinds of information, such as numbers, text, or lists. Each storage box has a **name**, which helps you find and use the information later in your code.

Think of a variable as a way to store a value you need to use again, such as the score in a game, a temperature reading, or the name of a person.

Why Are Variables Important?

Variables are one of the most fundamental parts of any programming language. They allow you to:

1. **Store Data**: You can store different types of data, like numbers or text, which you can use and change as needed.
2. **Reuse Values**: Instead of typing the same value repeatedly, you can store it in a variable and reuse it.
3. **Make Code Flexible**: Variables make your program more flexible. You can use them to write code that works with different values without changing the core logic.

Rules for Naming Variables

1. Start with a Letter or Underscore: Variable names should start with a letter (a-z, A-Z) or an underscore (_). For example, *score* or *_value*.
2. No Spaces: You cannot use spaces in variable names. Instead, use underscores (_) to separate words, like *player_score*.

3. Case-Sensitive: Variable names are **case-sensitive**, which means *temperature* and *Temperature* are considered different variables.
4. Descriptive Names: Use meaningful names for your variables to make your code easier to understand. For example, use *distance* instead of *d*.

Global Variables

What are Global Variables?
Global variables are variables that are declared outside of all functions and are accessible from any part of the program. Unlike local variables (which are only accessible within the function they are declared in), global variables can be used by any function in the program, making them useful for sharing data across multiple functions.

Why is Important
Global variables are used when you need a variable to be accessible throughout the entire program, across multiple functions. This is useful when different parts of the code need to share or update the same data, such as sensor values, counters, or configuration settings.

Syntax

```
global variableName
```

MicroPython Syntax Explanation
In MicroPython, global variables are declared similarly to Arduino. If you want to modify a global variable inside a function, you must use the *global* keyword within the function:

- *global variableName*: Tells the function to use the global version of the variable, not a local one.

Example

```
counter = 0 # Global variable
def increment_counter():
global counter # Access global variable
counter += 1
print(counter)
increment_counter()
increment_counter()
```

- The variable *counter* is declared globally, and the *increment_counter()* function modifies it using the *global* keyword.

Notes

- In MicroPython, global variables can be accessed from any function, but you need the *global* keyword if you want to modify their value inside a function.
- Just like in Arduino, global variables are initialized at the start of the program and retain their values throughout execution.

Warnings

- Overusing global variables can lead to confusion and potential errors if many parts of the program are modifying the same variables.
- Be careful when modifying global variables from within functions to avoid unintended side effects, especially in complex programs.

Local Variables

What are Local Variables?

Local variables are variables that are declared within a function or a block of code and are only accessible inside that specific function or block. Once the function finishes executing, the local variables are destroyed, and their values are no longer accessible.

Why is Important

Local variables are used when you only need a variable to store data temporarily within a specific function or block of code. They help avoid conflicts with global variables and ensure that the variable is only used in the context where it's needed.

Syntax Use

```
variableName = value
```

MicroPython Syntax Explanation

In MicroPython, local variables are declared within a function or block of code. They are used in the same way as in Arduino, but no explicit data type declaration is required:

- *variableName*: The name of the local variable.
- *value*: The initial value assigned to the variable.

Example

```
def my_function():
counter = 0 # Local variable
counter += 1
print(counter)
my_function()
my_function()
```

- Here, *counter* is a local variable inside the function *my_function()*. Every time the function is called, *counter* is reinitialized to 0 and incremented by 1.

Notes

- In MicroPython, local variables are automatically destroyed once the function execution is complete, similar to how they work in Arduino.
- Local variables make the code more modular and prevent variable conflicts across different parts of the program.

Warnings

- Like in Arduino, local variables in MicroPython are not preserved between function calls. If you need a variable to retain its value, consider using a global variable or passing it as a parameter.
- Avoid excessive use of local variables in deeply nested functions, as this can lead to memory issues on devices with limited resources.

Primitive Data Types:

1 . Intger variable int
What is
The `int` variable is a data type used to represent integer values in MicroPython. It allows you to store and manipulate whole numbers, which is essential for counting, indexing, and simple calculations.

Why is Important?
The `int` variable is crucial for basic operations such as loops, arithmetic, and indexing. Without integers, managing quantities, counting iterations, or accessing specific elements in a list becomes cumbersome.

Syntax
```
variable_name = int(value)
```

Syntax Explanation
variable_name represents the name you assign to store your integer value. *int(value)* assigns an integer value to the variable.

Code Example
```
temperature = int(25)
counter = int(0)
```

Notes
- You can use `int` to initialize a variable with any whole number.
- When converting from another data type to `int`, make sure the value is suitable for integer representation.

Warnings
- If you attempt to convert a non-numeric value to `int`, a `ValueError` may be raised.
- `int` variables cannot hold decimal numbers; use `float` if you need to work with fractional values.

2. Float Variable float

What is
A *float* variable is a type of data used in MicroPython to store numbers with decimals, like 23.5 or 3.14. You use *float* when you need to work with numbers that aren't whole, such as measurements or precise values.

Why is Important?
The *float* variable is important because it lets you do calculations with numbers that have decimals. This is useful when working with things like temperature, distances, or any situation where you need more precision than a whole number.

Syntax
```
variable_name = float(value)
```
Syntax Explanation
- *variable_name* is the name you give to your variable to store the number.
- *float(value)* means you are creating a decimal number, where *value* is the number you want to store.

Code Example
```
temperature = float(23.5)
distance = float(15.75)
```

Notes

- *float* is used to store numbers with decimals, allowing you to do more precise math.
- You can convert an integer to a *float* by using *float()*. For example, *float(5)* will become *5.0*.

Warnings

- Be careful when doing math with *float* values, because sometimes the result might not be exact due to how computers handle decimal numbers.
- Using *float* may take more memory than using whole numbers (*int*), so it's something to keep in mind when working on a microcontroller with limited space.

3. Bool Variable bool

What is

A *bool* variable is a type of data used in MicroPython that can only have one of two values: *True* or *False*. It is used when you need to represent something as being either on/off, yes/no, or true/false.

Why is Important?

The *bool* variable is important because it helps control decision-making in your program. For example, you can use it to determine if a condition is met or not, like checking if a button is pressed or if a temperature is above a certain level.

Syntax

```
variable_name = bool(value)
```

Syntax Explanation

- *variable_name* is the name you assign to the variable.
- *bool(value)* sets the variable to either *True* or *False*. You can also directly use *True* or *False* without converting another value.

Code Example

```
is_light_on = bool(True)
is_temperature_high = bool(False)
```

Notes

- You can also assign *True* or *False* directly without using *bool()*, like *is_valid = True*.
- *bool* is often used in conditional statements to control the flow of a program, like in *if* statements.

Warnings

- When converting other values to *bool*, remember that *0*, *None*, and empty sequences (like an empty string *""*) are considered *False*, while all other values are considered *True*.
- Be careful not to confuse *bool* with numerical values, as *True* is equivalent to *1* and *False* is equivalent to *0* in mathematical operations.

4. NoneType Variable None

What is
NoneType is a special data type in MicroPython that has only one possible value: *None*. It is used to represent the absence of a value or a "nothing" value. When a variable is assigned *None*, it means that it doesn't contain any useful information yet.

Why is Important?
NoneType is important because it allows you to define a variable that does not have a value yet. This can be useful when initializing variables before you assign them real data or when you need to indicate that no meaningful value exists.

Syntax
```
variable_name = None
```

Syntax Explanation

- *variable_name* is the name you assign to the variable.
- *None* is used to indicate that the variable currently has no value.

Code Example
```
temperature = None button_state = None
```
Notes
- You can use *None* to initialize a variable that will get a value later.
- Checking if a variable is *None* can be done using *if variable_name is None:*.

Warnings

- Do not use *None* in mathematical operations, as it will cause errors since it is not a number.
- When working with *NoneType*, be careful to handle it properly in conditions to avoid unexpected behavior in your code.

Sequence Data Types:

1. String Variable str

What is

A *str* variable is a type of data used in MicroPython to store text. A *str* (short for string) can hold a sequence of characters, such as letters, numbers, and symbols, all enclosed in quotation marks.

Why is Important?

The *str* variable is important because it allows you to work with text, like names, messages, or any information that involves characters. This is especially useful when displaying messages, taking user input, or interacting with text-based data.

Syntax

```
variable_name = str(value)
or variable_name = "text value"
```

Syntax Explanation

- *variable_name* is the name you give to the variable to store the text.
- *str(value)* converts a given value to a string.
- Alternatively, you can directly assign a string by using quotation marks like *"text value"*.

Code Example

```
name = str("John")
message = "Hello, World!"
```

Notes

- You can concatenate (join) two strings using the + operator, like *greeting = "Hello, " + "John"*.
- Strings can also be created by converting other data types, such as *str(123)* to get the text representation *"123"*.

Warnings

- Remember that numbers in a *str* format cannot be used in mathematical calculations unless you convert them back to an *int* or *float*.
- Be careful with quotation marks—always match the opening and closing quotation marks to avoid syntax errors.

2. List Variable list

What is
A *list* is a data type in MicroPython that allows you to store multiple values in a single variable. You can think of a *list* as a collection of items, such as numbers or strings, all enclosed in square brackets [ ].

Why is Important?
The *list* is important because it helps you store and manage multiple related values easily. For example, you could store the temperatures recorded at different times, or keep a list of names of users. This makes it easy to access, modify, or perform actions on the entire collection of items.

Syntax
```
variable_name = [value1, value2, value3, ...]
```

Syntax Explanation
- *variable_name* is the name you give to the list.
- The values inside the square brackets *[ ]* are the items in the list, separated by commas. They can be of any data type, like *int*, *float*, or *str*.

Code Example
```
temperatures = [23, 25, 21, 22]
names = ["Alice", "Bob", "Charlie"]
```

Notes
- You can access an item in the list using its index, like *temperatures[0]*, which would give you *23*.
- Lists are flexible; you can add items using *append()*, like *temperatures.append(26)*.

Warnings
- Indexing starts at *0*, not *1*. For example, *names[0]* gives *"Alice"*.
- If you try to access an index that doesn't exist, you'll get an *IndexError*. Always check the list's length with *len(list_name)* before accessing an index.

3. Tuple Variable tuple

What is
A *tuple* is a data type in MicroPython that allows you to store multiple values, similar to a list. However, unlike a list, the values in a *tuple* cannot be changed once they are set. A *tuple* is created by enclosing the values in parentheses *( )*.

Why is Important?
The *tuple* is important when you need to store a collection of items that should not be modified. This ensures that your data remains consistent and prevents accidental changes. For example, it is useful for storing fixed configuration settings or constant values.

Syntax
```
variable_name = (value1, value2, value3, ...)
```
Syntax Explanation
- *variable_name* is the name you assign to the tuple.
- The values inside the parentheses *( )* are the items in the tuple, separated by commas. These items can be of any data type, like *int*, *float*, or *str*.

Code Example
```
coordinates = (10, 20)
colors = ("red", "green", "blue")
```

Notes

- You can access an item in a tuple using its index, just like with a list, for example, *coordinates[0]* will give you *10*.
- Tuples can be used to store multiple values that should remain constant, which helps make your code safer and more predictable.

Warnings

- Tuples are immutable, which means you cannot change, add, or remove items after the tuple is created.
- If you need to modify the values, consider using a *list* instead of a *tuple*.

4. Bytes Variable bytes

What is
A *bytes* variable in MicroPython is a type of data used to represent sequences of bytes, which are numbers ranging from 0 to 255. It is commonly used when you need to work with binary data, such as reading data from sensors or working with communication protocols.

Why is Important?
The *bytes* type is important for low-level operations where you need precise control over the data, such as handling raw data from devices, working with communication interfaces (like UART or I2C), or storing data in a memory-efficient way.

Syntax

```
variable_name = bytes([value1, value2, ...])
```

Syntax Explanation
- *variable_name* is the name you give to the bytes variable.
- *bytes([value1, value2, ...])* creates a bytes object from the list of values, where each value is between 0 and 255.

Code Example

```
data = bytes([10, 20, 30])
message = b"Hello"
```

Notes
- You can create a *bytes* object directly by prefixing a string with *b*, like *b"Hello"*.
- The *bytes* type is immutable, which means you cannot change individual elements once the bytes object is created.

Warnings

- The values in a *bytes* object must be between 0 and 255. Trying to use a value outside this range will cause an error.
- Since *bytes* are immutable, if you need to modify the content, consider using a *bytearray*, which is a mutable version of *bytes*.

Set and Mapping Data Types:

1. Set Variable set

What is

A *set* is a data type in MicroPython that allows you to store a collection of unique values. Unlike lists or tuples, a *set* cannot have duplicate items, and the items are unordered, meaning their position is not fixed.

Why is Important?

The *set* is important when you need to store multiple unique items and don't want any duplicates. Sets are useful for operations like finding the union, intersection, or difference between collections of items, which can be helpful in various data-handling tasks.

Syntax

```
variable_name = {value1, value2, value3, ...}
```

Syntax Explanation

- *variable_name* is the name you give to the set.
- The values inside the curly braces *{ }* are the items in the set, separated by commas. The items can be of any data type, like *int*, *float*, or *str*.

Code Example

```
unique_numbers = {1, 2, 3, 4, 5}
unique_names = {"Alice", "Bob", "Charlie"}
```

Notes

- Sets are unordered, so the items do not have a specific index, and you cannot access elements using an index like with lists.
- You can add items to a set using the *add()* method, for example, *unique_numbers.add(6)*.

Warnings

- Sets cannot have duplicate values. If you add a duplicate, it will be ignored.
- Sets are not ordered, so the order of items may change when you add or remove elements, and you cannot rely on the order for accessing items.

2. Dictionary Variable dict

What is
A *dict* (short for dictionary) is a data type in MicroPython that stores data in key-value pairs. It works like a real-life dictionary, where each key has an associated value, making it easy to organize and access related data.

Why is Important?
The *dict* is important because it allows you to store and retrieve data efficiently using keys, which makes it easy to organize data that is related. For example, you can use a *dict* to store information like device configurations, sensor readings by their names, or any data that can be labeled.

Syntax

```
variable_name = {key1: value1, key2: value2, ...}
```

Syntax Explanation
- *variable_name* is the name you give to the dictionary.
- The keys and values are written in pairs inside curly braces { }, separated by a colon :. Multiple key-value pairs are separated by commas.

Code Example

```
person = {"name": "Alice", "age": 25, "city": "New York"}
sensor_readings = {"temperature": 23.5, "humidity": 60}
```

Notes
- You can access a value using its key, for example, *person["name"]* will give you *"Alice"*.
- You can add a new key-value pair by assigning a value to a new key, like *person["height"] = 170*.

Warnings
- Keys in a *dict* must be unique. If you use the same key again, it will overwrite the existing value.
- Be careful when accessing keys that might not exist, as it will raise a *KeyError*. You can use *get()* to avoid this, like *person.get("weight", "Not Available")*, which will return *"Not Available"* if the key does not exist.

Common Mistakes and How to Avoid Them

1. **Invalid Variable Names**
   - *Mistake*: Using a number at the start of the variable name or including spaces.
   - *How to Avoid*: Always start variable names with a letter or underscore. Replace spaces with underscores.
   - *Example*: Use *temperature_value* instead of *1temperature* or *temperature value*.
2. **Mismatching Data Types**
   - *Mistake*: Adding a string and a number.
   - *How to Avoid*: Convert data types before combining them.
   - *Example*: *print("Age: " + str(25))*.
3. **Not Initializing Variables**
   - *Mistake*: Using a variable without assigning it a value first.
   - *How to Avoid*: Always assign a value before using a variable.
   - *Example*: *count = 0* before *count = count + 1*.
4. **Reserved Keywords as Variable Names**
   - *Mistake*: Naming a variable with a reserved word like *print*, *if*, or *for*.
   - *How to Avoid*: Use descriptive names that are not reserved keywords.
   - *Example*: *temperature_reading* instead of *if*.
5. **Indexing Issues in Lists**
   - *Mistake*: Accessing an element from a list using an index that doesn't exist.
   - *How to Avoid*: Always check the list's length before accessing an index.
   - *Example*: *if len(numbers) > 2: print(numbers[2])*.

Chapter 5. Math Functions

This chapter introduces essential math functions provided by the *math* module in MicroPython. These functions are commonly used for mathematical and scientific calculations. The focus is on three key functions: *sqrt()*, *sin()*, and *cos()*.

Syntax Table

Topic	Syntax	Simple Example
Square Root	*math.sqrt(value)*	*math.sqrt(16) # Output: 4.0*
Sine	*math.sin(angle_radians)*	*math.sin(math.pi / 2) # Output: 1.0*
Cosine	*math.cos(angle_radians)*	*math.cos(math.pi / 3) # Output: 0.5*

Introduction to Math Functions

Math functions are essential for performing mathematical calculations in programming. In MicroPython, these functions are part of the math module, which includes common operations such as finding square roots, sine, cosine, and more. Below are some of the key functions provided by the math module and how they work.

Using the math Module:

1. Square Root Function sqrt()

What is
The *sqrt()* function is used in MicroPython to find the square root of a number. It returns a value that, when multiplied by itself, gives the original number.

Why is Important?

The *sqrt()* function is important for mathematical calculations where you need to determine the square root, which is common in geometry, physics, and many other scientific applications. It allows you to easily compute the square root without manually calculating it.

Syntax

```
math.sqrt(value)
```

Syntax Explanation

- *math* is the module that provides mathematical functions, so you need to import it first.
- *sqrt(value)* takes a number as input and returns its square root. *value* should be a non-negative number.

Code Example

```
import math result = math.sqrt(16)
print(result) # Output: 4.0
```

Notes

- Before using *sqrt()*, you must import the *math* module using *import math*.
- The result of *sqrt()* is a floating-point number, even if the input is a perfect square.

Warnings

- The *value* passed to *sqrt()* must be non-negative. If you pass a negative number, it will raise a *ValueError*.
- Ensure that the *math* module is properly imported; otherwise, attempting to use *sqrt()* will result in a *NameError*.

1. Sine Function sin()

What is

The *sin()* function in MicroPython is used to calculate the sine of an angle, which is a trigonometric function. It takes an angle in radians as input and returns the sine value, which is useful for working with waves, rotations, and periodic phenomena.

Why is Important?

The *sin()* function is important for various mathematical and engineering calculations, especially when dealing with oscillations, waveforms, or analyzing angles. It is commonly used in fields like physics, robotics, and electronics to model behavior like sensor readings or motor movement.

Syntax

```
math.sin(angle_in_radians)
```

Syntax Explanation

- *math* is the module that provides mathematical functions, so you need to import it first.
- *sin(angle_in_radians)* takes an angle in radians and returns the sine value of that angle.

Code Example

```
import math angle = math.pi / 2 sine_value = math.sin(angle)
print(sine_value) # Output: 1.0
```

Notes

- You must import the *math* module using *import math* to use the *sin()* function.
- The angle provided to *sin()* should be in radians. To convert degrees to radians, you can use *math.radians(degrees)*.

Warnings

- Be careful with the unit of the angle. The *sin()* function requires radians, not degrees.
- If you pass a very large value, you may experience precision issues due to how floating-point numbers are handled.

3. Cosine Function cos()

What is

The *cos()* function in MicroPython is used to calculate the cosine of an angle, which is a trigonometric function. It takes an angle in radians as input and returns the cosine value, which is useful for working with waveforms, angles, and periodic functions.

Why is Important?

The *cos()* function is important for calculations involving waveforms, rotations, or periodic behavior. It is frequently used in applications like robotics, signal processing, and physics to model or analyze scenarios involving angles and their relationships.

Syntax

```
math.cos(angle_in_radians)
```

Syntax Explanation

- *math* is the module that provides mathematical functions, so you need to import it first.
- *cos(angle_in_radians)* takes an angle in radians and returns the cosine value of that angle.

Code Example

```
import math angle = math.pi / 3 cosine_value = math.cos(angle)
print(cosine_value) # Output: 0.5
```

Notes

- You must import the *math* module using *import math* to use the *cos()* function.
- The angle given to *cos()* must be in radians. You can use *math.radians(degrees)* to convert degrees to radians if needed.

Warnings

- The input for the *cos()* function must be in radians, not degrees, to get the correct value.
- Using very large or very small values might result in precision issues due to the limitations of floating-point arithmetic in microcontrollers.

Common Mistakes and How to Avoid Them

1. **Not Importing the *math* Module**
   - **Mistake**: Forgetting to import the *math* module will result in a *NameError*.
   - **Solution**: Always include *import math* at the top of your script.
2. **Passing Negative Numbers to *sqrt()***
   - **Mistake**: Passing a negative number to *sqrt()* will raise a *ValueError*.
   - **Solution**: Ensure that the input to *sqrt()* is non-negative.

Chapter 6. Data Type Conversions

In MicroPython, it's common to need to convert between different data types, such as converting strings to numbers or vice versa. This is important for handling user input, performing calculations, or working with different forms of data. Below are three key functions used for type conversion: *int()*, *float()*, and *str()*.

Syntax Table

Topic	Syntax	Simple Example
Integer Conversion	*int(value)*	*int("42") # Output: 42*
Floating-Point Conversion	*float(value)*	*float("3.14") # Output: 3.14*
String Conversion	*str(value)*	*str(42) # Output: "42"*

Converting Between Types:

1. Integer Conversion Function int()

What is
The *int()* function in MicroPython is used to convert a value to an integer type. This means it will take a number or a string representing a number and convert it to a whole number (integer).

Why is Important?
The *int()* function is important because it allows you to convert other data types (like strings or floating-point numbers) into integers. This is essential when working with input values, calculations, or when you need to perform integer-based operations.

Syntax

```
int(value)
```

Syntax Explanation
- *value* can be a number or a string that represents a number. The *int()* function will convert this value to an integer.

Code Example

```
number_str = "42" number = int(number_str)
print(number) # Output: 42
float_value = 3.7 integer_value = int(float_value)
print(integer_value) # Output: 3
```

Notes
- If you use *int()* with a floating-point number, it will truncate the decimal part and return only the whole number.
- You can use *int()* with strings that represent valid whole numbers.

Warnings
- If the string value passed to *int()* is not a valid representation of an integer (e.g., *"abc"*), it will raise a *ValueError*.
- Using *int()* on a float will always round down, even if the decimal is greater than 0.5. For example, *int(4.9)* will result in *4*, not *5*.

2. Floating-Point Conversion Function float()

What is
The *float()* function in MicroPython is used to convert a value to a floating-point type, which is a number with a decimal point. It allows you to represent real numbers for more precision compared to integers.

Why is Important?
The *float()* function is important when working with values that require decimal precision, such as temperature measurements, distances, or financial calculations. It allows you to convert integers or strings into floating-point numbers for accurate mathematical operations.

Syntax

```
float(value)
```

Syntax Explanation

- *value* can be a number (integer) or a string representing a number. The *float()* function will convert this value to a floating-point number.

Code Example

```
number_str = "3.14" number = float(number_str)
print(number) # Output: 3.14
integer_value = 5 float_value = float(integer_value)
print(float_value) # Output: 5.0
```

Notes

- If you use *float()* with an integer, it will add a decimal point to create a floating-point number.
- You can use *float()* with strings that represent valid numbers, including those with decimals.

Warnings

- If the string value passed to *float()* is not a valid representation of a number (e.g., *"abc"*), it will raise a *ValueError*.
- Be mindful of precision issues when using floating-point numbers, as they can sometimes lead to rounding errors in calculations, especially with very large or very small values.

3. String Conversion Function str()

What is

The *str()* function in MicroPython is used to convert a value to a string type. It allows you to represent numbers, booleans, or other data as text, which is useful for displaying or processing data in a readable format.

Why is Important?

The *str()* function is important when you need to convert data to text format for output, user interaction, or storing information as strings. It is also helpful when you need to concatenate numbers with other strings to create meaningful messages.

Syntax

```
str(value)
```

Syntax Explanation
- *value* can be any data type, such as an integer, float, or boolean. The *str()* function will convert this value to a string.

Code Example

```
number = 42 number_str = str(number)
print(number_str) # Output: "42"
boolean_value = True boolean_str = str(boolean_value)
print(boolean_str) # Output: "True"
```

Notes
- You can use *str()* to easily concatenate different data types by converting them to strings first, such as *"The value is " + str(10)*.
- Using *str()* helps make non-text data readable and is useful for printing and logging information.

Warnings
- Be careful when converting complex data types, such as lists or dictionaries, into strings, as it might not be easily readable without formatting.
- When using *str()* on floating-point numbers, be aware of the precision, as it may include many decimal places depending on the value.

Common Mistakes and How to Avoid Them
1. **Not Handling Invalid Input for *int()* or *float()***
   - **Mistake**: Passing a string that cannot be converted to a number, like "abc", will raise a *ValueError*.
   - **Solution**: Always validate the input before converting it, or use exception handling (try-except) to catch errors.
2. **Using *int()* on Floating-Point Numbers**
   - **Mistake**: When using *int()* on floats, it truncates the decimal part, which may lead to unexpected results.
   - **Solution**: Be aware that *int()* always rounds down (truncates) rather than rounding.

Chapter 7. Operators and Expressions

This chapter focuses on **Operators and Expressions** in MicroPython. Operators allow you to perform arithmetic, comparison, and logical operations on values, helping you control the flow of your programs and perform essential calculations. We'll explore different types of operators, such as arithmetic operators, comparison operators, and logical operators, along with common mistakes and how to avoid them.

Syntax Table

Topic	Syntax	Simple Example
Addition	*value1 + value2*	*5 + 3 # Output: 8*
Subtraction	*value1 - value2*	*10 - 4 # Output: 6*
Multiplication	*value1 * value2*	*5 * 3 # Output: 15*
Division	*value1 / value2*	*10 / 2 # Output: 5.0*
Floor Division	*value1 // value2*	*10 // 3 # Output: 3*
Modulus	*value1 % value2*	*10 % 3 # Output: 1*
Exponentiation	*base ** exponent*	*2 ** 3 # Output: 8*
Equal To	*value1 == value2*	*5 == 5 # Output: True*
Not Equal To	*value1 != value2*	*5 != 3 # Output: True*
Greater Than	*value1 > value2*	*10 > 5 # Output: True*

Less Than	value1 < value2	3 < 7 # Output: True
Greater Than or Equal To	value1 >= value2	5 >= 5 # Output: True
Less Than or Equal To	value1 <= value2	4 <= 5 # Output: True
Logical AND	condition1 and condition2	True and False # Output: False
Logical OR	condition1 or condition2	True or False # Output: True
Logical NOT	not condition	not True # Output: False

Arithmetic Operators

Addition Operator (+)

What is

The addition operator + is used in MicroPython to add two values together. It can be used with numbers to perform arithmetic addition, or with strings to concatenate (join) them.

Why is Important?

The + operator is one of the basic arithmetic operations, and it is essential for performing calculations, combining numerical data, and building strings. It helps make mathematical operations easy and intuitive in your code.

Syntax

```
value1 + value2
```

Syntax Explanation

- *value1* and *value2* can be numbers (integers or floats) that you want to add, or strings that you want to concatenate.

Code Example

```
# Adding two numbers
result = 5 + 3
print(result) # Output: 8
# Concatenating two strings
greeting = "Hello, " + "World!"
print(greeting) # Output: "Hello, World!"
```

Notes
- The + operator can be used for both numbers and strings, but they must be compatible (i.e., you cannot add a number and a string directly).
- If you need to add a number to a string, convert the number to a string first using *str()*.

Warnings
- If you try to use + with incompatible types, such as an integer and a string without converting, it will raise a *TypeError*.
- When working with floating-point numbers, be aware of potential precision issues, especially when adding very large or very small values.

Subtraction Operator (-)

What is
The subtraction operator - is used in MicroPython to subtract one value from another. It is commonly used to perform arithmetic calculations involving differences between numbers.

Why is Important?
The - operator is crucial for performing arithmetic operations like finding the difference between two values. It is widely used in scenarios such as adjusting values, performing calculations in loops, or solving mathematical problems.

Syntax

```
value1 - value2
```

Syntax Explanation
- *value1* and *value2* are numbers (integers or floats) that you want to subtract, with *value2* being subtracted from *value1*.

Code Example

```
# Subtracting two numbers
result = 10 - 4
print(result) # Output: 6
# Using subtraction with variables
a = 15
b = 7
difference = a - b
print(difference) # Output: 8
```

Notes
- The - operator is used only for numerical values (integers or floats).
- You can use - to subtract a smaller value from a larger value to get a positive result, or vice versa to get a negative result.

Warnings
- If you use - with incompatible types (e.g., trying to subtract a number from a string), it will raise a *TypeError*.
- Be mindful of precision issues when working with floating-point numbers, as subtracting very large and very small values can lead to inaccuracies due to how floating-point arithmetic works.

Multiplication Operator (*)

What is
The multiplication operator * is used in MicroPython to multiply two values. It can be used with numbers to perform arithmetic multiplication, and also with strings to repeat them multiple times.

Why is Important?
The * operator is essential for performing multiplication in mathematical calculations, scaling values, or repeating strings. It helps simplify many types of arithmetic and data manipulation tasks in your code.

Syntax

```
value1 * value2
```

Syntax Explanation

- *value1* and *value2* can be numbers (integers or floats) that you want to multiply. You can also use *value1* with a string to repeat it multiple times, where *value2* must be an integer.

Code Example

```
# Multiplying two numbers
result = 5 * 3
print(result) # Output: 15
# Repeating a string multiple times
repeat_text = "Hi! " * 3
print(repeat_text) # Output: "Hi! Hi! Hi! "
```

Notes

- The * operator can be used to repeat strings by multiplying them with an integer. This is useful for creating repeated patterns or messages.
- When using the * operator with two numbers, both numbers can be either integers or floating-point values.

Warnings

- If you try to use the * operator with incompatible types (e.g., multiplying two strings), it will raise a *TypeError*.
- Be careful when multiplying very large numbers, as it can lead to overflow errors or memory issues, especially when working with limited resources like microcontrollers.

Division Operator (/)

What is

The division operator / is used in MicroPython to divide one value by another. It returns the result as a floating-point number, even if both operands are integers.

Why is Important?

The / operator is important for performing division operations in your code, which are fundamental in many mathematical calculations and data processing tasks. It allows you to calculate ratios, averages, and distribute values.

Syntax

```
value1 / value2
```

Syntax Explanation

- *value1* is the dividend (the number to be divided).
- *value2* is the divisor (the number by which you divide). The result will always be a floating-point number.

Code Example

```
# Dividing two numbers
result = 10 / 2
print(result) # Output: 5.0
# Using division with variables
a = 15
b = 4
division_result = a / b
print(division_result) # Output: 3.75
```

Notes

- Division with / always returns a floating-point number, even if both *value1* and *value2* are integers.
- For integer division (without a remainder), you can use the floor division operator //.

Warnings

- Dividing by zero will raise a *ZeroDivisionError*. Always ensure *value2* is not zero before performing division.
- Be cautious with floating-point precision, as dividing very large or very small numbers may lead to inaccuracies due to how floating-point arithmetic is handled.

Floor Division Operator (//)

What is

The floor division operator // is used in MicroPython to divide one value by another and return the largest integer less than or equal to the result. This means it performs a division and then rounds down to the nearest whole number.

Why is Important?

The // operator is important when you need to perform integer division without worrying about the remainder or fractional part. It is particularly useful in situations where only whole numbers are required, such as indexing or dividing items into even parts.

Syntax

```
value1 // value2
```

Syntax Explanation
- *value1* is the dividend (the number to be divided).
- *value2* is the divisor (the number by which you divide). The result will be an integer.

Code Example

```
# Floor dividing two numbers
result = 10 // 3
print(result) # Output: 3
# Using floor division with variables
a = 15
b = 4
floor_division_result = a // b
print(floor_division_result) # Output: 3
```

Notes
- The *//* operator discards the remainder and returns only the integer part of the division.
- If either operand is a float, the result will also be a float but without the fractional part (e.g., *15.0 // 4* gives *3.0*).

Warnings
- Dividing by zero will raise a *ZeroDivisionError*. Always check that *value2* is not zero before performing floor division.
- Be careful when using negative numbers, as the result will be rounded down towards negative infinity, which may not always match your expectations.

Modulus Operator (%)
What is
The modulus operator % is used in MicroPython to find the remainder when one value is divided by another. It is useful for determining if a number is evenly divisible by another number.

Why is Important?
The % operator is important for operations where you need to check if a value is divisible (e.g., checking for even or odd numbers) or when working with cyclic patterns like determining whether a number is within a range or finding remainders.

Syntax

```
value1 % value2
```

Syntax Explanation

- *value1* is the dividend (the number to be divided).
- *value2* is the divisor (the number by which you divide). The result is the remainder after the division.

Code Example

```
# Finding the remainder of two numbers
remainder = 10 % 3
print(remainder) # Output: 1
# Using modulus with variables
a = 15
b = 4
remainder_result = a % b
print(remainder_result) # Output: 3
```

Notes

- The % operator is helpful for determining if a number is even or odd. For example, *number % 2* gives *0* for even numbers and *1* for odd numbers.
- You can also use the modulus operator to work with cyclic conditions, such as checking the rotation index within a given range.

Warnings

- Dividing by zero will raise a *ZeroDivisionError*. Always ensure *value2* is not zero before using the modulus operator.
- The result of % will have the same sign as the divisor, so be careful when working with negative numbers, as it can affect the remainder.

Exponentiation Operator ()**
What is

The exponentiation operator ** is used in MicroPython to raise one number to the power of another. It performs exponential calculations, where a base number is multiplied by itself a specified number of times.

Why is Important?
The ** operator is important for performing mathematical calculations that involve powers, such as squaring a number or finding higher powers. It is especially useful in applications involving scientific calculations, physics, and geometry.

Syntax

```
base ** exponent
```

Syntax Explanation

- *base* is the number you want to raise.
- *exponent* is the power to which you want to raise the base. The result will be *base* raised to the power of *exponent*.

Code Example

```
# Calculating the power of a number
result = 2 ** 3
print(result) # Output: 8
# Using exponentiation with variables
base = 5
exponent = 2
power_result = base ** exponent
print(power_result) # Output: 25
```

Notes

- The ** operator can be used with both integers and floats, allowing for fractional exponents (e.g., *9 ** 0.5* calculates the square root of *9*).
- You can also use negative exponents to calculate the reciprocal of a number raised to a positive power (e.g., *2 ** - 3* results in *0.125*).

Warnings

- Be cautious when using very large exponents, as the result can quickly grow beyond the storage capacity of your microcontroller, leading to an *OverflowError*.
- When using negative bases with fractional exponents, you may encounter complex numbers, which MicroPython may not handle directly without additional libraries or functions.

Comparison Operators

Equal To Operator (==)

What is
The == operator in MicroPython is used to compare two values to check if they are equal. It returns *True* if the values are the same, and *False* otherwise.

Why is Important?
The == operator is important for making decisions in your code. It is used in conditional statements, such as *if* statements, to determine whether certain actions should be taken based on whether two values are equal.

Syntax

```
value1 == value2
```

Syntax Explanation
- *value1* and *value2* are the values you want to compare. They can be of any data type, such as numbers, strings, or booleans.

Code Example

```
# Comparing two numbers
result = (5 == 5)
print(result) # Output: True
# Using equal to in an if statement
temperature = 25
if temperature == 25:
print("Temperature is 25 degrees.") # Output: Temperature is 25
degrees.
```

Notes
- The == operator checks for value equality, not identity. This means it checks if the values are the same, not whether they are stored in the same memory location.
- The result of == is always a boolean (*True* or *False*), and it can be used in any context that expects a boolean value.

Warnings
- Be careful not to confuse the == operator with the assignment operator =, which is used to assign values to variables.

Not Equal To Operator (!=)

What is
The *!=* operator in MicroPython is used to compare two values to check if they are not equal. It returns *True* if the values are different, and *False* if they are the same.

Why is Important?
The *!=* operator is important for decision-making in your code. It is used in conditional statements to determine whether certain actions should be taken based on whether two values are not equal.

Syntax

```
value1 != value2
```

Syntax Explanation
- *value1* and *value2* are the values you want to compare. They can be of any data type, such as numbers, strings, or booleans.

Code Example

```
# Comparing two numbers
result = (5 != 3)
print(result) # Output: True
# Using not equal to in an if statement
password = "abc123"
if password != "password":
print("Access Denied.") # Output: Access Denied.
```

Notes
- The *!=* operator checks for value inequality, meaning it verifies if the values are different.
- The result of *!=* is always a boolean (*True* or *False*), which can be used in *if* statements or loops to control the flow of your program.

Warnings
- Be careful when comparing different data types, as this can lead to unexpected results. For example, *5 != "5"* will return *True* because one is an integer and the other is a string.
- Avoid confusing the *!=* operator with the assignment operator =, which is used to assign values to variables.

Greater Than Operator (>)

What is
The > operator in MicroPython is used to compare two values to check if the first value is greater than the second. It returns *True* if the first value is larger, and *False* otherwise.

Why is Important?
The > operator is important for decision-making and conditional logic in your code. It is useful for comparing numerical values to determine if one is larger than the other, which is helpful in sorting, filtering, or controlling the flow of your program.

Syntax

```
value1 > value2
```

Syntax Explanation
- *value1* and *value2* are the values you want to compare. Both can be integers, floats, or any other comparable data type.

Code Example

```
# Comparing two numbers
result = 10 > 5
print(result) # Output: True
# Using greater than in an if statement
speed = 60
if speed > 50:
print("You are over the speed limit!") # Output: You are over the speed
limit!
```

Notes
- The > operator can be used with both integers and floats.
- This operator is often used in *if* statements, loops, or to sort values by comparing them.

Warnings
- Be careful when comparing different data types, such as strings and numbers, as it can lead to errors or unexpected results.
- If you compare two values that are not directly comparable (like a string and an integer), it will raise a *TypeError*. Always ensure the data types are compatible before comparing them.

Less Than Operator (<)

What is
The < operator in MicroPython is used to compare two values to check if the first value is less than the second. It returns *True* if the first value is smaller, and *False* otherwise.

Why is Important?
The < operator is important for making comparisons and implementing conditional logic in your code. It is useful for situations where you need to verify if one value is smaller than another, such as setting limits, filtering data, or controlling loops.

Syntax

```
value1 < value2
```

Syntax Explanation
- *value1* and *value2* are the values you want to compare. Both can be integers, floats, or any other comparable data type.

Code Example

```
# Comparing two numbers
result = 3 < 7
print(result) # Output: True
# Using less than in an if statement
temperature = 18
if temperature < 20:
print("It's a bit cold today.") # Output: It's a bit cold today.
```

Notes
- The < operator works with numbers (integers or floats) and helps in determining the relationship between them.
- It is commonly used in *if* statements, loops, and conditional checks.

Warnings
- Be careful not to compare incompatible data types, such as trying to compare a string with a number, as it can cause a *TypeError*.
- When comparing values, ensure the types are consistent to avoid unexpected outcomes or errors.

Greater Than or Equal To Operator (>=)

What is
The >= operator in MicroPython is used to compare two values to check if the first value is greater than or equal to the second. It returns *True* if the first value is either greater than or equal to the second value, and *False* otherwise.

Why is Important?
The >= operator is important for making comparisons and implementing decision-making logic in your code. It is useful for scenarios where you need to determine if a value has reached or exceeded a specific threshold, which is common in control flow and condition checks.

Syntax

```
value1 >= value2
```

Syntax Explanation
- *value1* and *value2* are the values you want to compare. Both can be integers, floats, or any other comparable data type.

Code Example

```
# Comparing two numbers
result = 5 >= 5
print(result) # Output: True
# Using greater than or equal to in an if statement
score = 75
if score >= 70:
print("You passed the exam!") # Output: You passed the exam!
```

Notes
- The >= operator checks both conditions—whether the first value is greater than or equal to the second.
- It is commonly used in loops, conditionals, and comparisons involving thresholds.

Warnings
- Be mindful of the data types being compared, as comparing incompatible types (like a string and a number) will raise a *TypeError*.
- Ensure that the values are of a comparable type to avoid unexpected results or runtime errors.

Less Than or Equal To Operator (<=)

What is
The <= operator in MicroPython is used to compare two values to check if the first value is less than or equal to the second. It returns *True* if the first value is either less than or equal to the second value, and *False* otherwise.

Why is Important?
The <= operator is important for implementing conditions and decision-making in your code. It is useful when you need to determine if a value is below or has reached a certain limit, which is commonly used in loops and conditional checks.

Syntax

```
value1 <= value2
```

Syntax Explanation
- *value1* and *value2* are the values you want to compare. Both can be integers, floats, or any other comparable data type.

Code Example
```
# Comparing two numbers
result = 4 <= 5
print(result) # Output: True
# Using less than or equal to in an if statement
temperature = 22
if temperature <= 25:
print("Temperature is comfortable.") # Output: Temperature is
comfortable.
```

Notes
- The <= operator checks both conditions—whether the first value is less than or equal to the second.
- This operator is often used in loops, conditionals, and checks where there is a limit or maximum threshold.

Warnings
- Avoid comparing incompatible data types, like a string with a number, as this will raise a *TypeError*.
- Always ensure that the values being compared are of a compatible type to avoid unexpected outcomes or errors during program execution.

Logical Operators

Logical AND Operator (and)

What is
The *and* operator in MicroPython is a logical operator used to combine two conditions. It returns *True* only if both conditions are *True*, and returns *False* if either of the conditions is *False*.

Why is Important?
The *and* operator is important for making complex logical decisions in your code. It allows you to check multiple conditions simultaneously, which is useful for scenarios where more than one condition must be met before proceeding with a specific action.

Syntax
```
condition1 and condition2
```

Syntax Explanation
- *condition1* and *condition2* are the two conditions being checked. Both must be *True* for the result to be *True*; otherwise, the result will be *False*.

Code Example
```
# Checking two conditions
temperature = 20
humidity = 50
if temperature > 15 and humidity < 60:
print("The weather is pleasant.") # Output: The weather is pleasant.
```

Notes
- The *and* operator is used to ensure that multiple criteria are met before taking an action.
- It is commonly used in *if* statements, loops, or other decision-making constructs to combine conditions.

Warnings
- If either condition is *False*, the entire expression will be *False*. Make sure both conditions are defined and evaluated properly to avoid unexpected outcomes.
- Be careful with data types; logical conditions should be boolean expressions or values that can be evaluated as *True* or *False*.

Logical OR (or)

What is
The *or* operator in MicroPython is a logical operator used to combine two conditions. It returns *True* if at least one of the conditions is *True*, and only returns *False* if both conditions are *False*.

Why is Important
The *or* operator is crucial for decision-making when you need to verify if at least one condition is met. It simplifies logic in scenarios where multiple conditions can trigger an action, making it essential for controlling the flow of your program.

Syntax

```
condition1 or condition2
```

Syntax Explanation
condition1 and *condition2* are the two conditions being checked. The result is *True* if either one of the conditions is *True*. It will only be *False* if both conditions are *False*.

Code Example

```
temperature = 10 humidity = 70 if temperature < 15 or humidity > 65:
print("The weather is not ideal.")
```

Notes
- The *or* operator is useful when at least one condition should be satisfied before executing a block of code.
- It can be used in *if* statements or loops to simplify decision-making where multiple possibilities exist.

Warnings
- If both conditions are *False*, the entire expression will be *False*. Ensure your conditions are well defined.
- Be cautious with data types; logical conditions should be boolean expressions or values that can be evaluated as *True* or *False*.

Logical NOT (not)

What is
The *not* operator in MicroPython is a logical operator used to reverse the truth value of a condition. If a condition is *True*, the *not* operator will make it *False*, and vice versa.

Why is Important
The *not* operator is important for situations where you need to negate a condition. It helps simplify logic in cases where you want to perform an action when a condition is *False* rather than *True*.

Syntax

```
not condition
```

Syntax Explanation
not is placed before a condition, and it will return the opposite boolean value of that condition. If the condition is *True*, *not condition* will return *False*, and if it is *False*, *not condition* will return *True*.

Code Example

```
is_button_pressed = False if not is_button_pressed:
print("Button is not pressed.")
```

Notes
- The *not* operator is used when you want to reverse the outcome of a condition.
- It is commonly used in *if* statements or loops where the opposite condition is required.

Warnings
- Be careful with double negatives (using *not* too many times), as they can make the logic harder to understand.
- Ensure that the condition is properly defined to avoid unexpected results when using *not*.

Common Mistakes and How to Avoid Them

1. **Using Incompatible Data Types with Operators**
   - ○ **Mistake**: Trying to add a string and an integer without converting the integer to a string, resulting in a *TypeError*.
   - ○ **Solution**: Convert the integer to a string using *str()* before concatenating, e.g., *"Age: " + str(age)*.
2. **Dividing by Zero**
   - ○ **Mistake**: Dividing a number by zero will raise a *ZeroDivisionError*.
   - ○ **Solution**: Always check that the divisor is not zero before performing the division.
3. **Precision Issues with Floating-Point Arithmetic**
   - ○ **Mistake**: Relying on exact values when using floating-point numbers can lead to inaccuracies, especially with very small or large values.
   - ○ **Solution**: Be mindful of precision limitations with floating-point numbers and avoid expecting exact values.
4. **Misusing the Comparison Operators**
   - ○ **Mistake**: Confusing the assignment operator (=) with the equality operator (==), leading to incorrect comparisons.
   - ○ **Solution**: Ensure you use == for comparisons and = for assignment.
5. **Neglecting Logical Operator Precedence**
   - ○ **Mistake**: Misunderstanding the precedence of logical operators can lead to unexpected results in complex expressions.
   - ○ **Solution**: Use parentheses to clarify the intended order of operations in compound logical expressions.

Chapter 8. Control Structures

Control structures in MicroPython allow you to control how your program behaves under different conditions. This chapter covers essential concepts like conditional statements, loops, and error handling, which help you write dynamic and responsive programs.

Syntax Table

Topic	Syntax	Simple Example
If Statement	if condition:	if x > 10: print("x is greater")
Elif Statement	elif condition:	elif x == 10: print("x is equal to 10")
Else Statement	else:	else: print("x is less than 10")
For Loop	for variable in sequence:	for i in range(5): print(i)
While Loop	while condition:	while x < 10: x += 1
Break	break	for i in range(10): if i == 5: break
Continue	continue	for i in range(5): if i == 3: continue
Pass	pass	for i in range(5): pass
Return	return value	def add(a, b): return a + b
Try-Except Block	try: except ExceptionType:	try: result = 10/0 except ZeroDivisionError: print("Cannot divide!")

Conditional Statements:

If Statement

What is
The *if* statement in MicroPython is a conditional statement used to execute a block of code if a specified condition is *True*. If the condition is *False*, the code block is skipped.

Why is Important
The *if* statement is essential for decision-making in your program. It allows you to control the flow of the code by performing actions only when certain conditions are met, making your program responsive and dynamic.

Syntax

```
if condition:
# code block
```

Syntax Explanation
if condition checks whether the condition is *True* or *False*. If it is *True*, the indented code block will run. If the condition is *False*, the code block will be skipped.

Code Example

```
temperature = 30 if temperature > 25:
print("It's hot today.")
```

Notes
- The *if* statement is used to control which parts of your code are executed based on certain conditions.
- Indentation is crucial in MicroPython for defining the code block that belongs to the *if* statement.

Warnings
- Be careful with indentation. Improper indentation can lead to syntax errors or unexpected behavior.
- Ensure that the condition inside the *if* statement is properly defined to avoid errors or incorrect logic.

Elif

What is

The *elif* statement in MicroPython is short for "else if." It allows you to check multiple conditions in sequence after an *if* statement. If the *if* condition is *False*, the *elif* condition is checked. This continues until a condition is *True* or all conditions are evaluated.

Why is Important

The *elif* statement is important because it allows you to handle multiple scenarios in your code efficiently. Instead of writing multiple *if* statements, you can use *elif* to make your code cleaner and easier to manage, especially when checking for several conditions.

Syntax

```
if condition1:
# code block
elif condition2:
# code block
else:
# code block
```

Syntax Explanation

- *if condition1*: The first condition is checked. If it's *True*, the code block under it runs.
- *elif condition2*: If the *if* condition is *False*, this condition is checked. If *True*, the code block under it runs.
- *else*: If none of the previous conditions are *True*, this final block is executed.

Code Example

```
temperature = 20 if temperature > 30:
        print("It's hot.")
elif temperature > 15:
        print("It's warm.")
else:
        print("It's cool.")
```

Notes

- The *elif* statement is optional, but useful when multiple conditions need to be evaluated.
- You can include as many *elif* statements as needed between *if* and *else*.

Warnings

- Ensure that only one condition is *True* at a time; if multiple conditions are *True*, only the first one encountered will be executed.

Else

What is
The *else* statement in MicroPython is used as a fallback option in conditional statements. It is executed when all preceding *if* or *elif* conditions are *False*.

Why is Important
The *else* statement is important because it ensures that a block of code will always run if none of the conditions in the *if* or *elif* statements are met. This provides a way to handle cases that don't fit specific conditions.

Syntax

```
if condition:
# code block
else:
# code block
```

Syntax Explanation
- *if condition*: The first condition is checked. If it's *True*, the code block under *if* is executed.
- *else*: If the *if* condition is *False*, the *else* block is executed, serving as a default case.

Code Example
```
temperature = 10 if temperature > 20:
print("It's warm.")
else:
print("It's cold.")
```

Notes
- The *else* statement is optional but useful when you want to ensure that some code runs, even if none of the *if* or *elif* conditions are satisfied.
- The *else* block always comes at the end of an *if-elif-else* chain.

Warnings
- Ensure that the *else* block is properly indented to avoid syntax errors.
- The *else* block will run only when all other conditions are *False*. Make sure the logic fits your program's needs.

Looping

For

What is
The *for* loop in MicroPython is used to iterate over a sequence (like a list, tuple, or range) and execute a block of code for each element in that sequence.

Why is Important
The *for* loop is important because it allows you to repeat a block of code multiple times without having to write it out for each iteration. This is useful for tasks like processing data, running repetitive tasks, or automating actions in your program.

Syntax

```
for variable in sequence:
# code block
```

Syntax Explanation
- *for variable*: This part defines a variable that takes the value of each item in the sequence one at a time.
- *in sequence*: This is the sequence you are iterating over, such as a list, tuple, or range.
- The code block will be executed once for each item in the sequence.

Code Example

```
for i in range(5):
print(i)
```

This will print the numbers 0 to 4.

Notes
- The *for* loop is commonly used to iterate over a list of items or run a block of code a specific number of times.
- The *range()* function is often used to generate a sequence of numbers.

Warnings
- Be careful with sequences that are too large, as looping over large data sets might affect performance on limited-memory microcontrollers.

While

What is
The *while* loop in MicroPython is a control flow statement that repeatedly executes a block of code as long as a specified condition remains *True*.

Why is Important
The *while* loop is important because it allows you to run a block of code multiple times based on a condition. It's useful for situations where you don't know in advance how many iterations are needed, but you want the loop to continue until a specific condition is met.

Syntax

```
while condition:
# code block
```

Syntax Explanation
- *while condition*: The loop runs as long as the condition is *True*.
- The code block will execute repeatedly until the condition becomes *False*.

Code Example

```
counter = 0 while counter < 5:
print(counter)
counter += 1
```

This will print numbers from 0 to 4.

Notes
- The *while* loop is useful when you don't know how many times the loop should run and want it to continue until a condition is no longer met.
- Be sure to update the condition inside the loop to eventually stop the loop, or it will run indefinitely.

Warnings
- Be careful with infinite loops. If the condition never becomes *False*, the loop will keep running and may crash your microcontroller.

Break and Continue Statement

Break Statement

What is
The *break* statement in MicroPython is used to exit a loop prematurely, before it has gone through all its iterations or met its condition.

Why is Important
The *break* statement is important because it allows you to stop a loop when a certain condition is met, providing greater control over the loop's execution. This is useful when you want to stop a loop based on dynamic conditions.

Syntax

```
break
```

Syntax Explanation
The *break* statement can be placed inside a *for* or *while* loop. When the loop encounters the *break* statement, it immediately stops, and the program continues with the code following the loop.

Code Example

```
for i in range(10):
if i == 5:
break print(i)
```

This will print numbers 0 to 4, and then stop when *i* equals 5.

Notes
- The *break* statement is useful for ending loops early when a specific condition is met.
- You can use *break* in both *for* and *while* loops.

Warnings
- Be cautious when using *break* as it can make your loops exit unexpectedly, especially if the condition that triggers it isn't properly defined.
- Overuse of *break* statements may make your code harder to follow, so use them sparingly and only when necessary.

Continue Statement

What is
The *continue* statement in MicroPython is used to skip the current iteration of a loop and move on to the next iteration. It does not exit the loop; instead, it bypasses the remaining code for the current iteration.

Why is Important
The *continue* statement is important when you want to skip certain iterations in a loop based on specific conditions. It allows you to fine-tune the execution of your loops by skipping over unwanted cases without stopping the loop entirely.

Syntax

```
continue
```

Syntax Explanation
The *continue* statement is placed inside a *for* or *while* loop. When encountered, it causes the loop to immediately proceed to the next iteration, skipping any code below the *continue* statement for that iteration.

Code Example

```
for i in range(5):
if i == 3:
continue print(i)
```

This will print the numbers 0, 1, 2, 4, skipping 3.

Notes
- The *continue* statement is useful when you want to skip specific iterations of a loop but still want the loop to continue running.
- It helps in cases where you want to avoid certain conditions without exiting the loop.

Warnings
- Overuse of *continue* can make the loop logic harder to follow. Use it only when necessary to maintain code readability.

Pass and Return Statement

What is

The *pass* statement in MicroPython is a placeholder that does nothing when executed. It is used when a statement is syntactically required but no action is needed.

Why is Important

The *pass* statement is important for structuring code without causing syntax errors. It allows you to create empty blocks of code, which can be useful when planning or writing functions, loops, or classes that will be implemented later.

Syntax

```
pass
```

Syntax Explanation

The *pass* statement can be placed inside any block of code, such as loops, functions, or conditionals, where Python expects a statement but you don't want to perform any actions.

Code Example

```
for i in range(5):
pass
```

This loop does nothing but is valid.

Notes

- The *pass* statement is often used as a placeholder while developing code. It lets you focus on writing other parts of your program without causing errors.
- You can use *pass* in functions, loops, or conditionals when you don't need them to perform any action for now.

Warnings

- *pass* doesn't perform any operation, so be careful not to forget to replace it with meaningful code in the final version of your program.

Return Statement

What is
The *return* statement in MicroPython is used in functions to send a value back to the caller. Once the *return* statement is executed, the function terminates, and the specified value is passed back.

Why is Important
The *return* statement is important because it allows functions to provide results or output that can be used later in the program. It enables functions to process data and return a specific value or result.

Syntax

```
return value
```

Syntax Explanation
The *return* statement is used inside a function. It can return a value (such as an integer, string, list, etc.), or it can return nothing (by simply using *return* without any value).

Code Example

```
def add_numbers(a, b):
return a + b
result = add_numbers(3, 5)
print(result) # Output: 8
```

Notes
- The *return* statement can return any type of data, including numbers, strings, lists, or even other functions.
- A function can have multiple *return* statements, but only one will be executed based on the function's logic.

Warnings
- Once the *return* statement is executed, the function ends, so no code after *return* will run.
- Be cautious when using multiple *return* statements in a function, as it can make the code harder to follow.

Exception Handling
What is
Exception handling in MicroPython refers to the process of managing errors that occur during program execution, preventing the program from crashing. It allows you to catch and handle unexpected situations, ensuring the program can respond gracefully to errors.

Why is Important
Exception handling is important because it helps in writing robust and error-tolerant code. By catching and managing errors, your program can avoid unexpected crashes and continue running or provide meaningful error messages to the user.

Syntax

```
try:
# code that might raise an exception
except ExceptionType:
# code to handle the exception
```

Syntax Explanation
- *try*: The code inside this block is executed, and it may raise an exception.
- *except*: If an error (exception) occurs in the *try* block, the *except* block runs to handle the error.
- *ExceptionType* is optional and specifies the type of error to catch (e.g., ValueError, ZeroDivisionError). If omitted, it catches any exception.

Code Example

```
try:
result = 10 / 0 except ZeroDivisionError:
print("Cannot divide by zero!")
```

This will catch the division error and print a message instead of crashing the program.

Notes
- Exception handling is useful when dealing with unpredictable situations, like user input or file handling.
- You can use multiple *except* blocks to handle different types of exceptions.

Warnings
- Be careful not to catch generic exceptions without handling them properly, as it may hide bugs or make debugging harder.
- Always aim to catch specific exceptions (e.g., *ValueError, FileNotFoundError*) to handle different cases effectively.

Common Mistakes and How to Avoid Them

1. **Improper Indentation**
   - **Mistake**: Forgetting to indent code within *if, for, while,* or *try* blocks.
   - **How to Avoid**: Ensure all code under control structures is indented with 4 spaces. *if x > 10: print("x is greater") – Wrong: no indentation.*
2. **Incorrect Condition Syntax**
   - **Mistake**: Using the wrong comparison operator (e.g., *x = 10* instead of *x == 10*).
   - **How to Avoid**: Always use == to check for equality in conditions. *if x = 10: – Wrong: should use == for equality.*
3. **Infinite Loops**
   - **Mistake**: Not updating the condition in a *while* loop, causing it to run indefinitely.
   - **How to Avoid**: Ensure that the condition changes during the loop. *counter = 0; while counter < 5: print(counter) – Wrong: no update to counter.*

Chapter 9. Timing and Delays

Timing is a crucial aspect of programming, especially in embedded systems and IoT projects. Whether you're waiting for a sensor to provide accurate readings, controlling an LED to blink at regular intervals, or handling multitasking with background operations, timing functions like *time.sleep()* and non-blocking timers are essential tools.

Syntax Table

Topic	Syntax	Simple Example
Blocking Delay	*time.sleep(seconds)*	*import time; time.sleep(2)*
Non-blocking Timer	*Timer.init(period=milliseconds, mode, callback=function)*	*timer.init(period=1000, mode=Timer.PERIODIC, callback=my_function)*
Stopping a Timer	*timer.deinit()*	*timer.deinit()*

Using time.sleep() for Creating Delays

What is
The *time.sleep()* function in MicroPython is used to pause the execution of a program for a specified amount of time. It is commonly used to introduce delays between operations.

Why is Important
time.sleep() is important because it allows you to control the timing of your program, which can be essential for tasks like sensor reading, LED blinking, or creating timed intervals in your code.

Syntax

```
time.sleep(seconds)
```

Syntax Explanation
- *time.sleep()* is the function call.
- *seconds* is the number of seconds the program should wait before continuing. This can be a floating-point number to create sub-second delays (e.g., *time.sleep(0.5)* for half a second).

Code Example

```
import time print("Start")
time.sleep(2)
print("End")
```

This will print "Start," wait for 2 seconds, and then print "End."

Notes
- You can use *time.sleep()* to create pauses in your program for both whole and fractional seconds.
- It's often used in loops to control the pace of repeated actions like blinking LEDs or polling sensors.

Warnings
- Be cautious when using long delays, as they can make your program unresponsive for that duration.
- *time.sleep()* halts the entire program, so if you need other parts of the program to continue running during a delay, consider other timing techniques.

Non-blocking Delays Using Timers

What is

Non-blocking delays using timers in MicroPython allow you to create delays without stopping the execution of your entire program. Timers run in the background while the main program continues, making them useful for multitasking.

Why is Important

Non-blocking delays are important because they enable your program to handle multiple tasks simultaneously. Unlike *time.sleep()*, which blocks the entire program, timers let you perform other actions while waiting, which is crucial for real-time applications like sensor data reading and controlling devices.

Syntax

```
Timer.init(period=milliseconds, mode=Timer.ONE_SHOT or Timer.PERIODIC,
callback=function)
```

Syntax Explanation

- *Timer.init()* is used to set up the timer.
- *period* specifies the interval in milliseconds.
- *mode* defines how the timer operates: *Timer.ONE_SHOT* for a single delay or *Timer.PERIODIC* for repeated intervals.
- *callback* is the function that will be executed once the timer finishes.

Code Example

```
from machine import Timer def blink_led(timer):
print("LED blink")
timer = Timer(0)
timer.init(period=1000, mode=Timer.PERIODIC, callback=blink_led)
```

This example will call the *blink_led* function every 1 second without blocking the main program.

Notes

- Timers are ideal for non-blocking delays where you need periodic actions, such as sensor polling or blinking LEDs, while still allowing the rest of the program to run.
- You can stop a timer using *timer.deinit()* when it is no longer needed.

Warnings

- Be careful with overlapping timers; ensure that multiple timers do not interfere with each other.
- Always properly handle the *callback* function to avoid unexpected behavior when the timer triggers.

Common Mistakes and How to Avoid Them

1. **Blocking the Entire Program with *time.sleep()***
   - **Mistake**: Using *time.sleep()* for long delays, causing your program to become unresponsive.
   - **How to Avoid**: Limit the use of *time.sleep()* to short delays or use non-blocking timers when multitasking is required. *import time; time.sleep(10) – This will halt the program for 10 seconds, making it unresponsive during that time.*

Chapter 10. Functions and Modules

Functions are a fundamental part of any programming language, and in MicroPython, they help organize your code, making it more reusable, readable, and easier to maintain. Functions allow you to encapsulate code that performs specific tasks, making your programs more efficient. In this chapter, you'll learn how to create functions, use parameters, return values, and explore more advanced topics like default parameters, keyword arguments, and variable scope.

Syntax Table

Topic	Syntax	Simple Example
Function Definition	*def function_name(parameters):*	*def greet(name): print("Hello, " + name)*
Function with Return Value	*def function_name(parameters): return value*	*def add(a, b): return a + b*
Function with Default Param	*def function_name(param1 =value1):*	*def greet(name, message="Hello"): print(message + ", " + name)*
Function Call	*function_name(arguments)*	*greet("Alice")*

Creating and Using Functions

What is

A function in MicroPython is a reusable block of code that performs a specific task. You define a function once and can call it as many times as needed throughout your program.

Why is Important

Functions are important because they help organize and simplify your code. Instead of writing the same code repeatedly, you can call a function whenever you need to perform a task. This not only makes your code more efficient but also easier to read and maintain.

Syntax

```
def function_name(parameters):
# code block
```

Syntax Explanation

- *def*: Keyword used to define a function.
- *function_name*: The name you give to the function.
- *parameters*: Optional inputs (arguments) that you can pass to the function to process.
- The indented *code block* inside the function is executed when the function is called.

Code Example

```
def greet(name):
print("Hello, " + name)
greet("Alice")
greet("Bob")
```

This will print "Hello, Alice" and "Hello, Bob."

Notes

- Functions can take parameters, allowing you to customize their behavior based on the inputs provided.
- You can also return a value from a function using the *return* statement.

Warnings

- Ensure that the function is defined before calling it, otherwise, you'll encounter a *NameError*.
- Passing the wrong number of arguments or incorrect types may result in a *TypeError*, so be careful with parameter handling.

Function Parameters and Return Values

What is

Function parameters are variables defined in a function that allow you to pass data into the function. Return values are the outputs of a function that can be sent back to the calling code after the function has executed.

Why is Important

Parameters allow functions to be more flexible by accepting different inputs, which makes the function reusable in various contexts. Return values are important because they allow functions to provide results, making them useful for processing data and performing calculations.

Syntax

```
def function_name(param1, param2, ...):
# code block
return value
```

Syntax Explanation

- *param1, param2, ...*: These are placeholders for the inputs that the function accepts.
- *return value*: The function ends and sends back the specified result to the caller.

Code Example

```
def add_numbers(a, b):
return a + b
result = add_numbers(3, 7)
print(result) # Output: 10*
```

Notes

- You can define multiple parameters in a function to make it work with different inputs.
- The *return* statement allows you to send back results from the function to the rest of the program.

Warnings

- If a function does not have a *return* statement, it returns *None* by default.
- Be cautious with the number and type of parameters passed to the function to avoid errors.

Default Parameters and Keyword Arguments

What is
In MicroPython, functions can have default parameters, which provide a default value if no argument is passed. Keyword arguments allow you to specify arguments by name when calling a function, making the function calls more readable.

Why is Important
Default parameters are important because they make functions more flexible and versatile by allowing some arguments to be optional. Keyword arguments improve code readability and make it easier to understand the purpose of each argument when calling a function.

Syntax

```
def function_name(param1=value1, param2=value2):
# code block
```

Syntax Explanation
- *param1=value1*: This defines a parameter with a default value. If no value is provided when the function is called, the default is used.
- When calling the function, you can specify the arguments using *param1=value1* to make the code clearer.

Code Example

```
def greet(name, message="Hello"):
print(message + ", " + name)
greet("Alice") # Output: Hello, Alice
greet("Bob", "Hi") # Output: Hi, Bob
```

Notes
- Default parameters must be defined after any required parameters (i.e., non-default ones).
- You can mix positional and keyword arguments when calling a function.

Warnings
- Be careful when mixing default and non-default parameters—non-default ones should come first in the function definition.

Understanding Scope

What is

Scope in MicroPython refers to the region of a program where a variable is accessible. Return values are the results that a function sends back to the code that called it using the *return* statement.

Why is Important

Understanding scope is important because it determines where variables can be used within your program, preventing errors caused by referencing undefined variables. Return values are crucial for getting output from functions, enabling you to use the result elsewhere in your code.

Syntax

```
def function_name():
# code block
return value
```

Syntax Explanation

- Variables defined inside a function have *local scope*, meaning they can only be used within that function.
- The *return* statement allows you to send a value back from a function to the part of the program that called it.

Code Example

```
def calculate_sum(a, b):
result = a + b # result has local scope
return result
total = calculate_sum(5, 10)
print(total) # Output: 15
```

Notes

- Variables defined inside a function (local variables) are not accessible outside the function.
- Return values allow you to pass data out of a function to be used in other parts of your program.

Warnings

- Be careful with variable scope: if you need to access a value outside of a function, you must return it using the *return* statement.

Using Built-in and External Modules

What is

Modules in MicroPython are collections of pre-written code that provide additional functionality to your program. Built-in modules are included in MicroPython by default, while external modules can be added as needed to extend capabilities.

Why is Important

Using modules is important because they allow you to leverage existing code to perform common tasks, saving time and effort. Modules like *time*, *machine*, and *network* offer essential functions for controlling hardware, managing time, or connecting to the internet, making your development faster and easier.

Syntax

```
import module_name from module_name import function_name
```

Syntax Explanation

- *import module_name*: This imports the entire module, allowing access to all its functions and classes.
- *from module_name import function_name*: This imports only specific functions or classes from a module.

Code Example

```
import time time.sleep(2) # Pauses execution for 2 seconds
from math import sqrt print(sqrt(16)) # Output: 4.0
```

Notes

- Built-in modules like *time*, *math*, and *machine* provide essential functions that are ready to use.
- External modules can be added via the MicroPython package manager (mpy) or manually uploaded to your ESP32/ESP8266 device.

Warnings

- Ensure external modules are compatible with MicroPython before using them.

Installing and Managing External Modules

What is
External modules in MicroPython are additional libraries that are not included by default but can be installed or manually uploaded to your ESP32/ESP8266 device to extend its functionality. These modules provide specialized functions that may not be available in built-in modules.

Why is Important
Installing external modules is important because it allows you to add advanced functionality to your MicroPython projects, such as working with sensors, communication protocols, or other peripherals. This flexibility is essential for building more complex and feature-rich applications.

Syntax

```
upip.install('module_name')
```

Syntax Explanation
- *upip.install('module_name')*: This is the command used to install external modules using the MicroPython package installer. It fetches the module from a repository and installs it onto your device.

Code Example

```
import upip upip.install('micropython-umqtt.robust') # Installs the
MQTT library for handling IoT protocols
```

Notes
- You can use *upip* to install packages directly on your ESP32/ESP8266 if it's connected to the internet.
- Alternatively, you can manually upload external modules to your device using tools like *ampy* or *Thonny*.

Warnings
- Make sure your ESP32/ESP8266 is connected to the internet if you're using *upip* for installation.

Working with the `machine` Module for Hardware Control

What is

The *machine* module in MicroPython provides access to low-level hardware features of microcontrollers, such as GPIO pins, ADC (analog-to-digital converters), PWM (pulse-width modulation), and other peripherals. It allows you to interact directly with hardware components connected to your ESP32 or ESP8266.

Why is Important

The *machine* module is important because it enables you to control hardware like sensors, actuators, and displays. By using the *machine* module, you can interface with the physical world, making your MicroPython project capable of controlling devices, reading data, and responding to external inputs.

Syntax

```
from machine import Pin, ADC, PWM
```

Syntax Explanation

- *Pin*: This class is used to control GPIO pins for input/output operations.
- *ADC*: This class is used to read analog values from pins (e.g., sensors).
- *PWM*: This class allows you to generate pulse-width modulation signals for controlling devices like motors or LEDs.

Code Example

```
from machine import Pin led = Pin(2, Pin.OUT) # Configures GPIO2 as an
output pin
led.on() # Turns the LED on
led.off() # Turns the LED off*
```

Notes

- The *machine* module is essential for controlling hardware components directly from your MicroPython code.
- You can use it to manage GPIO pins for both input and output, read analog data, or generate PWM signals for controlling brightness, speed, or other variables.

Using the network Module for Wi-Fi Connectivity

What is

The *network* module in MicroPython allows you to connect your ESP32 or ESP8266 to Wi-Fi networks. It provides the tools to configure and manage network interfaces (such as Wi-Fi), making it essential for IoT applications that require internet access.

Why is Important

The *network* module is important because it enables your device to connect to a Wi-Fi network, allowing you to send and receive data over the internet. This is crucial for creating IoT projects where the device communicates with web servers, cloud platforms, or other networked devices.

Syntax

```
import network sta_if = network.WLAN(network.STA_IF)
sta_if.active(True)
sta_if.connect('SSID', 'password')
```

Syntax Explanation

- *network.WLAN()*: Creates a WLAN (Wi-Fi) interface.
- *network.STA_IF*: Sets the device to "station" mode, allowing it to connect to an existing Wi-Fi network.
- *active(True)*: Activates the Wi-Fi interface.
- *connect('SSID', 'password')*: Connects to the specified Wi-Fi network using the provided SSID and password.

Code Example

```
import network sta_if = network.WLAN(network.STA_IF)
sta_if.active(True)
sta_if.connect('Your_SSID', 'Your_Password')
while not sta_if.isconnected():
pass # Wait for connection
print('Connected to Wi-Fi:', sta_if.ifconfig())
```

This example connects the device to a Wi-Fi network and prints the IP address once connected.

Notes

- The *network* module allows you to configure both station mode (STA_IF) for connecting to Wi-Fi and access point mode (AP_IF) for creating a hotspot.
- You can use *sta_if.isconnected()* to check whether the device is successfully connected to the Wi-Fi network.

Warnings

- Ensure that the SSID and password are correct, or the device will not connect to the network.
- Avoid using hardcoded credentials in your code for security reasons. Consider using environment variables or secure methods to handle sensitive information.

Using the dht Module for Temperature and Humidity Sensors

What is

The *dht* module in MicroPython is used to interface with DHT11 and DHT22 sensors, which are commonly used for measuring temperature and humidity. This module simplifies reading data from these sensors connected to your ESP32 or ESP8266.

Why is Important

The *dht* module is important because it provides an easy way to retrieve temperature and humidity data from sensors in your projects. This is essential for applications such as weather stations, environmental monitoring, or home automation systems.

Syntax

```
import dht from machine import Pin sensor = dht.DHT11(Pin(pin_number))
or sensor = dht.DHT22(Pin(pin_number))
```

Syntax Explanation

- *dht.DHT11()* or *dht.DHT22()*: Initializes the DHT11 or DHT22 sensor connected to a specific GPIO pin.
- *Pin(pin_number)*: Specifies the pin to which the sensor is connected.
- *sensor.measure()*: Reads the data from the sensor.
- *sensor.temperature()*: Returns the temperature in Celsius.
- *sensor.humidity()*: Returns the humidity percentage.

Code Example

```
import dht from machine import Pin
sensor = dht.DHT11(Pin(14)) # Initialize DHT11 sensor on GPIO 14
sensor.measure() # Trigger a measurement
temperature = sensor.temperature() # Get temperature in Celsius
humidity = sensor.humidity() # Get humidity percentage
print("Temperature:", temperature, "°C")
print("Humidity:", humidity, "%")
```

Notes

- The *dht* module works with both DHT11 and DHT22 sensors. DHT11 is less accurate but cheaper, while DHT22 provides better accuracy and a wider range.
- Be sure to use the correct sensor initialization (*DHT11* or *DHT22*) based on the model you're using.

Warnings

- DHT sensors are relatively slow and can only be read every 2 seconds (for DHT11) or 0.5 seconds (for DHT22). Make sure you wait between consecutive reads.
- Ensure that the sensor is wired correctly, with the right pin for data, power, and ground to avoid errors in data readings.

Common Mistakes and How to Avoid Them

1. **Not Defining the Function Before Calling It**
   - **Mistake**: Calling a function before it's defined.
   - **How to Avoid**: Ensure that the function definition is placed before any function calls in the code. *greet("Alice") # Error: function not defined yet.*
2. **Incorrect Number of Arguments**
   - **Mistake**: Passing too few or too many arguments to a function, causing a *TypeError*.
   - **How to Avoid**: Ensure that the function is called with the correct number of arguments. *def greet(name): print("Hello, " + name) – Calling greet() without arguments will raise an error.*
3. **Not Using Return Values Properly**
   - **Mistake**: Forgetting to use the *return* statement in functions that need to send data back.
   - **How to Avoid**: Always use *return* when a function needs to send a result back to the calling code. *def add(a, b): a + b # Incorrect: missing return statement.*

Chapter 11. GPIO I/O operations

GPIO (General Purpose Input/Output) pins are vital in microcontroller projects, allowing you to interface with external hardware such as LEDs, buttons, sensors, and motors. In MicroPython, setting up and controlling GPIO pins enables your ESP32 or ESP8266 to interact with the physical world. This chapter covers setting up GPIO pins for input and output, handling digital and analog signals, using PWM for precise control, and implementing interrupts for real-time responses.

Syntax Table

Topic	Syntax	Simple Example
GPIO Pin Setup (Output)	*from machine import Pin* *pin = Pin(pin_number, Pin.OUT)*	*led = Pin(2, Pin.OUT)* *led.on()*
GPIO Pin Setup (Input)	*pin = Pin(pin_number, Pin.IN)*	*button = Pin(0, Pin.IN)* *if button.value() == 0:* *print("Button pressed")*
Digital Input with Pull-up	*pin = Pin(pin_number, Pin.IN, Pin.PULL_UP)*	*button = Pin(0, Pin.IN, Pin.PULL_UP)*
Analog Input	*from machine import ADC, Pin* *adc = ADC(Pin(pin_number))*	*adc = ADC(Pin(34))* *value = adc.read()*
PWM Output	*from machine import PWM, Pin* *pwm = PWM(Pin(pin_number), freq=freq, duty=duty)*	*pwm = PWM(Pin(2), freq=5000)* *pwm.duty(512)*

GPIO Interrupts	pin.irq(trigger=Pin.IRQ_FALLING, handler=function_name)	button.irq(trigger=Pin.IRQ_FALLING, handler=button_pressed)

GPIO Pin Setup

What is
GPIO (General Purpose Input/Output) pins are digital pins on your ESP32 or ESP8266 that can be configured as inputs or outputs. They are used to interface with hardware components such as LEDs, buttons, sensors, and motors.

Why is Important
Setting up GPIO pins is important because it allows you to control or read external components from your MicroPython code. This is essential for building interactive systems where your microcontroller needs to respond to sensors or control devices.

Syntax

```
from machine import Pin pin = Pin(pin_number, Pin.OUT) or pin =
Pin(pin_number, Pin.IN)
```

Syntax Explanation
- *Pin(pin_number, Pin.OUT)*: Sets the pin to output mode, used for controlling devices like LEDs or motors.
- *Pin(pin_number, Pin.IN)*: Sets the pin to input mode, used for reading sensors or button states.
- *pin.on()*: Turns on the output (for output mode).
- *pin.off()*: Turns off the output (for output mode).
- *pin.value()*: Reads the pin value (for input mode).

Code Example

```
from machine import Pin
led = Pin(2, Pin.OUT) # Set GPIO2 as an output pin
led.on() # Turn on the LED
led.off() # Turn off the LED*
button = Pin(0, Pin.IN) # Set GPIO0 as an input pin
if button.value() == 0: # Check if the button is pressed
print("Button pressed")
```

Notes

- GPIO pins can be used to control digital devices or read digital inputs (on/off states).
- Be sure to configure the pin correctly for input or output depending on the task.

Warnings

- Always verify the correct GPIO pin numbers for your board as they can differ between ESP32 and ESP8266.
- Be careful with voltage levels, as certain components may require specific operating voltages. Overvoltage can damage your board or components.

Reading GPIO Input

Digital Input: machine.Pin()

What is

The *machine.Pin()* function in MicroPython is used to set up a GPIO pin as a digital input to detect signals like button presses or sensor outputs. Digital inputs read binary states: high (1) or low (0).

Why is Important

Setting up digital inputs is important because it allows your ESP32 or ESP8266 to sense external signals, such as detecting when a button is pressed or when a sensor is triggered. This is essential for interactive or automated systems.

Syntax

```
from machine import Pin pin = Pin(pin_number, Pin.IN, Pin.PULL_UP or
Pin.PULL_DOWN)
pin.value()
```

Syntax Explanation

- *Pin(pin_number, Pin.IN)*: Configures the pin as a digital input.
- *Pin.PULL_UP or Pin.PULL_DOWN*: Optional internal resistor settings to prevent floating inputs.
- *pin.value()*: Reads the current state of the pin (1 for high, 0 for low).

Code Example

```
from machine import Pin button = Pin(0, Pin.IN, Pin.PULL_UP) # Setup
GPIO0 as input with internal pull-up resistor*
if button.value() == 0: # Check if button is pressed (active low)
print("Button pressed")*
else:
print("Button not pressed")
```

Notes
- Pull-up or pull-down resistors are crucial for stable digital input readings, especially for buttons. These resistors prevent "floating" states when no signal is connected.
- The *Pin.PULL_UP* and *Pin.PULL_DOWN* options set the internal resistors, making external resistors unnecessary in many cases.

Warnings
- Ensure the input signal's voltage level is compatible with the ESP32/ESP8266's 3.3V GPIO pins to avoid damage.
- Avoid using floating inputs without resistors, as they may produce unreliable or fluctuating readings.

Analog Input: machine.ADC()

What is
The *machine.ADC()* function in MicroPython is used to read analog signals from components like sensors. Unlike digital inputs, which can only read high (1) or low (0) states, analog inputs read a range of values that represent continuous signals, such as temperature or light levels.

Why is Important
Analog input is important because it allows your ESP32 or ESP8266 to interpret real-world signals, like varying voltage levels from sensors. This is essential for projects where you need to monitor environmental conditions, such as temperature, light, or pressure.

Syntax

```
from machine import ADC, Pin adc = ADC(Pin(pin_number))
```

Syntax Explanation

- *ADC(Pin(pin_number))*: Initializes an analog-to-digital converter (ADC) on a specific GPIO pin.
- *adc.read()*: Reads the analog value from the pin, returning a value between 0 and 4095 (for ESP32), representing the voltage level.

Code Example

```
from machine import ADC, Pin adc = ADC(Pin(34)) # Set GPIO34 for analog
input*
value = adc.read() # Read analog value*
print("Analog value:", value)
```

Notes

- The ESP32 can read analog values between 0 and 4095 (corresponding to 0V to 3.3V by default). On ESP8266, the range is typically 0 to 1023.
- You can scale the analog value to match the sensor's range or voltage reference using simple math, e.g., *voltage = (value / 4095) * 3.3*.

Warnings

- Ensure that the input voltage to the analog pin does not exceed the operating voltage (typically 3.3V for ESP32 and ESP8266). Higher voltages may damage the board.
- The ADC input resolution may vary depending on the pin and board model, so check your microcontroller's specifications to ensure accurate readings.

Writing to GPIO Output

Digital Output: machine.Pin().value()

What is

The *machine.Pin().value()* function in MicroPython is used to set a GPIO pin as a digital output. This allows your ESP32 or ESP8266 to control external devices like LEDs, motors, or relays by sending either a high (1) or low (0) signal.

Why is Important

Digital outputs are essential for controlling hardware components. By configuring a GPIO pin as an output, you can interact with various external devices, making your project capable of driving components like lights, buzzers, or motors.

Syntax

```
from machine import Pin pin = Pin(pin_number, Pin.OUT)
pin.value(value)
```

Syntax Explanation

- *Pin(pin_number, Pin.OUT)*: Sets the pin as an output pin.
- *pin.value(value)*: Sets the pin's output value. A value of *1* sets the pin to high (on), and *0* sets it to low (off).

Code Example

```
from machine import Pin led = Pin(2, Pin.OUT) # Set GPIO2 as an output*
led.value(1) # Turn on the LED*
led.value(0) # Turn off the LED*
```

Notes

- The *value(1)* function sets the GPIO pin to high, and *value(0)* sets it to low.
- You can use this method to control devices like LEDs, relays, or any other digital output devices.

Warnings

- Be cautious of the voltage and current ratings when controlling external components, especially high-power devices like motors or relays.
- Ensure that external components are properly wired to prevent damage to your microcontroller and components. Always use appropriate transistors or relays for high-power devices.

PWM Output: machine.PWM()

What is

The *machine.PWM()* function in MicroPython is used to generate Pulse Width Modulation (PWM) signals on a GPIO pin. PWM allows you to control devices like LEDs, motors, and servos by adjusting the duty cycle of the signal, which determines how long the pin stays high within a cycle.

Why is Important

PWM output is important because it provides fine control over devices. By adjusting the duty cycle, you can control brightness, motor speed, or even position in servos, allowing for more precise and dynamic interactions in your project.

Syntax

```
from machine import PWM, Pin pwm = PWM(Pin(pin_number), freq=frequency,
duty=duty_cycle)
```

Syntax Explanation

- *PWM(Pin(pin_number), freq=frequency)*: Initializes a PWM signal on a specific GPIO pin with the given frequency (in Hz).
- *duty=duty_cycle*: Sets the duty cycle of the PWM signal. The value ranges from 0 (always off) to 1023 (always on) for ESP8266 and 0 to 65535 for ESP32.

Code Example

```
from machine import PWM, Pin pwm = PWM(Pin(2), freq=5000) # Set GPIO2
with 5kHz PWM signal*
pwm.duty(512) # Set duty cycle to 50% (on for half the time)*
```

Notes

- The frequency determines how fast the signal oscillates. For example, a 5kHz frequency will oscillate the signal 5000 times per second.
- The duty cycle controls how long the signal stays high in each cycle. For example, 50% duty means the signal is high for half of the cycle.

GPIO Pull-Up and Pull-Down Resistors

What is

Pull-up and pull-down resistors are internal or external resistors used to ensure that a GPIO pin has a defined state (either high or low) when it is not actively driven by an external signal. A pull-up resistor pulls the pin to a high state, while a pull-down resistor pulls it to a low state.

Why is Important

Pull-up and pull-down resistors are important because they prevent floating states (undefined or noisy signals) on GPIO pins, which can lead to erratic behavior. This is especially useful when working with buttons or switches where the pin needs a reliable state when not pressed or toggled.

Syntax

```
from machine import Pin pin = Pin(pin_number, Pin.IN, Pin.PULL_UP) or
pin = Pin(pin_number, Pin.IN, Pin.PULL_DOWN)
```

Syntax Explanation

- *Pin(pin_number, Pin.IN)*: Configures the pin as an input.
- *Pin.PULL_UP*: Enables the internal pull-up resistor, setting the pin to a default high state.
- *Pin.PULL_DOWN*: Enables the internal pull-down resistor, setting the pin to a default low state.

Code Example

```
from machine import Pin button = Pin(0, Pin.IN, Pin.PULL_UP) #
Configure GPIO0 as input with a pull-up resistor*
if button.value() == 0: # Check if the button is pressed (active low)
print("Button pressed")*
```

Notes

- Pull-up and pull-down resistors are useful for buttons or switches where you want to ensure a stable signal when no input is present.
- Most GPIO pins on ESP32 and ESP8266 support internal pull-up and pull-down resistors, so external resistors are often unnecessary.

Warnings

- Be cautious when using pull-down resistors, as not all GPIO pins on the ESP32/ESP8266 support internal pull-down resistors. Check the pinout for your specific board.

GPIO Interrupts

What is

GPIO interrupts allow your ESP32 or ESP8266 to react immediately to changes on a GPIO pin (e.g., a button press) by executing a specific function when the state of the pin changes. Interrupts can trigger on rising edges (low to high), falling edges (high to low), or both.

Why is Important

GPIO interrupts are important because they enable real-time reactions to hardware events without constantly checking the pin's state. This makes your code more efficient by only executing when an event occurs, rather than using continuous polling, which can waste processing time.

Syntax

```
pin.irq(trigger=Pin.IRQ_FALLING or Pin.IRQ_RISING,
handler=function_name)
```

Syntax Explanation

- *pin.irq()*: Sets up an interrupt request (IRQ) on a GPIO pin.
- *trigger=Pin.IRQ_FALLING*: The interrupt will trigger on a falling edge (high to low).
- *trigger=Pin.IRQ_RISING*: The interrupt will trigger on a rising edge (low to high).
- *handler=function_name*: Specifies the function to execute when the interrupt is triggered.

Code Example

```
from machine import Pin def button_pressed(pin):
print("Button was pressed")
button = Pin(0, Pin.IN, Pin.PULL_UP)
button.irq(trigger=Pin.IRQ_FALLING, handler=button_pressed) # Interrupt
on button press*
```

Notes

- Interrupts are useful for events like button presses, sensor triggers, or any other situation where you need an immediate response without continuous polling.

- You can use either *IRQ_FALLING* (for detecting a low transition) or *IRQ_RISING* (for detecting a high transition), or even both with *IRQ_RISING | IRQ_FALLING*.

Warnings

- Avoid placing long or blocking code in the interrupt handler, as it can slow down or freeze your program. Keep the handler function short and simple.
- Be cautious with shared resources (like global variables) in interrupts, as they may cause conflicts or unexpected behavior without proper handling or synchronization.

Common Mistakes and How to Avoid Them

1. **Incorrect GPIO Pin Setup**
   - ○ **Mistake**: Using incorrect pin numbers or failing to set the pin to input or output mode.
   - ○ **How to Avoid**: Always verify the correct pin number for your specific board and ensure the pin is set to the correct mode (input/output). *led = Pin(2, Pin.OUT) – Check the pinout for your board.*
2. **Floating Inputs Without Pull-up or Pull-down Resistors**
   - ○ **Mistake**: Failing to use pull-up or pull-down resistors with input pins, leading to unreliable readings.
   - ○ **How to Avoid**: Use *Pin.PULL_UP* or *Pin.PULL_DOWN* for stable input readings when no signal is connected. *button = Pin(0, Pin.IN, Pin.PULL_UP) – Prevents floating states.*
3. **Exceeding Voltage Limits**
   - ○ **Mistake**: Applying more than 3.3V to GPIO pins on ESP32/ESP8266, which can damage the board.
   - ○ **How to Avoid**: Ensure the voltage levels of connected components do not exceed the board's operating voltage (typically 3.3V). *adc = ADC(Pin(34)) – Ensure the sensor voltage is 3.3V or lower.*

Chapter 12.Programming Fundamentals Project

Working with GPIO Pins

Project-1 : Button-Controlled LED with ESP32/ESP8266 Using MicroPython

Object:
This project demonstrates how to work with GPIO pins in MicroPython by applying variables, data types, and control structures to turn an LED on or off based on a button press. The LED will blink, and the button will control its state.

Programming Fundamentals name
- *Variables and Data Types*: Variables are used to define the GPIO pin numbers for both the LED and the button. This ensures flexibility if you need to change pin assignments.
- *int*: We use the *int* data type to store GPIO pin numbers, allowing us to easily manage pin configuration in the program.
- *Control Structures (if-else, while)*:
    - *if-else*: We use *if-else* to check the button's state and determine whether the LED should be turned on or off.
    - *while*: The *while* loop is used to continuously monitor the button's state and allow real-time interaction.

Use Syntax
- *Pin(pin_number, Pin.OUT)*: Used to configure the GPIO pin as an output for controlling the LED.
- *Pin(pin_number, Pin.IN, Pin.PULL_UP)*: Used to configure the GPIO pin as an input with a pull-up resistor for reading the button state.
- *if condition:*: Used to check if the button is pressed or not, and control the LED accordingly.
- *while condition:*: Creates a continuous loop to monitor the button press and control the LED.

Requirement component:

- ESP32 or ESP8266
- LED
- Button
- Resistors (220Ω for LED, 10kΩ if using an external pull-up resistor)
- Breadboard
- Jumper wires

Circuit diagram:

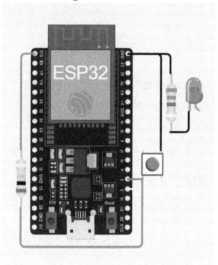

Circuit connection:

- Connect the LED's positive leg (anode) to GPIO 2 (for example) via a 220Ω resistor, and connect the negative leg (cathode) to GND.
- Connect one side of the button to GPIO 0, and the other side to GND. If using an external pull-up resistor, connect a 10kΩ resistor between GPIO 0 and 3.3V.

Micropython code

```
from machine import Pin
import time

led_pin = 2 # Define LED GPIO pin (int)
button_pin = 0 # Define button GPIO pin (int)
led = Pin(led_pin, Pin.OUT)
button = Pin(button_pin, Pin.IN, Pin.PULL_UP)

while True:
    if button.value() == 0: # Button pressed (active low)
        led.on() # Turn on the LED
    else:
        led.off() # Turn off the LED
        time.sleep(0.1) # Debounce delay
```

Code Explanation

- *led_pin = 2, button_pin = 0*: These variables store the pin numbers for the LED and button using the *int* data type, making it easy to manage and modify pin numbers.
- *Pin(led_pin, Pin.OUT)*: Configures the GPIO pin for the LED as an output.
- *Pin(button_pin, Pin.IN, Pin.PULL_UP)*: Configures the GPIO pin for the button as an input with an internal pull-up resistor to avoid floating values when the button is not pressed.
- *if button.value() == 0*: Checks if the button is pressed. The button is active low, so when pressed, its value is 0.
- *led.on()* and *led.off()*: These control the LED by turning it on or off based on the button's state.
- *time.sleep(0.1)*: Introduces a short delay to debounce the button, ensuring stable and reliable input readings.

Note:

- The GPIO pin numbers (e.g., 2 for the LED and 0 for the button) can be changed depending on your board and setup.
- The pull-up resistor ensures that the button works reliably without needing external hardware components, but you can also use an external pull-up resistor if needed.

Project -2: Controlling Multiple LEDs with a Button Using ESP32/ESP8266 and MicroPython

Object:

This project demonstrates how to control multiple LEDs using a single button in MicroPython, incorporating variables, control structures, and lists to manage the states of multiple LEDs. When the button is pressed, the LEDs will toggle sequentially.

Programming Fundamentals name

- *Variables and Data Types*: We use variables to define the GPIO pin numbers for multiple LEDs and the button. Lists are used to store multiple pin numbers.
- *int*: Used to define GPIO pin numbers for LEDs and the button.
- *Lists*: A list is used to store and manage the LED pins for easy control in a loop.
- *Control Structures (if-else, while)*:
  - *if-else*: Checks the button's state and toggles the LEDs based on that.
  - *while*: Continuously monitors the button press to control the LEDs over time.

Use Syntax

- *Pin(pin_number, Pin.OUT)*: Defines the GPIO pins for the LEDs as outputs.
- *Pin(pin_number, Pin.IN, Pin.PULL_UP)*: Defines the GPIO pin for the button as an input with a pull-up resistor.
- *if condition:*: Used to check the button's state.
- *while condition:*: Creates a loop for continuous LED control and button monitoring.
- *list.append(value)*: Adds LED pin numbers to the list for easier management in a loop.

Requirement component:

- ESP32 or ESP8266
- 3 LEDs
- Button
- Resistors (220Ω for each LED, 10kΩ if using an external pull-up resistor)
- Breadboard
- Jumper wires

Circuit diagram:

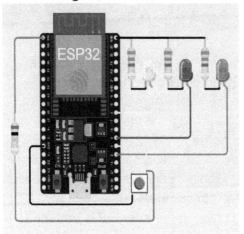

Circuit connection:

- Connect each LED's positive leg (anode) to a separate GPIO pin (e.g., GPIO 2, GPIO 4, and GPIO 5) through a 220Ω resistor. Connect each LED's negative leg (cathode) to GND.
- Connect one side of the button to GPIO 0, and the other side to GND. If using an external pull-up resistor, connect a 10kΩ resistor between GPIO 0 and 3.3V.

Micropython code

```
from machine import Pin
import time

led_pins = [2, 4, 5]  # Define GPIO pins for 3 LEDs using a list
button_pin = 0        # Define button GPIO pin
leds = [Pin(pin, Pin.OUT) for pin in led_pins]  # Initialize LEDs
button = Pin(button_pin, Pin.IN, Pin.PULL_UP)
led_index = 0         # To track which LED to toggle

while True:
    if button.value() == 0:  # Button pressed (active low)
        leds[led_index].on()   # Turn on the current LED
        time.sleep(0.5)        # Keep the LED on for a short period
        leds[led_index].off()  # Turn off the current LED
        led_index = (led_index + 1) % len(leds)  # Move to the next LED
        time.sleep(0.5)        # Debounce delay

    time.sleep(0.1)  # Short delay to prevent rapid button reading
```

Code Explanation

- *led_pins = [2, 4, 5]*: A list that stores the GPIO pin numbers for the three LEDs.
- *Pin(pin, Pin.OUT) for pin in led_pins*: Initializes each LED as an output based on the list of GPIO pins.
- *if button.value() == 0*: Checks if the button is pressed.
- *leds[led_index].on() and leds[led_index].off()*: Turn on and off the current LED in the sequence.
- *led_index = (led_index + 1) % len(leds)*: Moves to the next LED in the list, using the modulo operator to cycle back to the first LED after the last one.
- *time.sleep(0.5)*: Adds delays for debounce and to give visible feedback of the LED toggling.

Note:

- You can increase the number of LEDs by adding more pin numbers to the *led_pins* list.
- The button press toggles through each LED, and the LEDs blink sequentially with each button press. You can adjust the time delay and cycle behavior based on your project's needs.

Sensors and Actuators

Project-1 : Button-Controlled LED with Temperature Sensor Feedback Using ESP32/ESP8266 and MicroPython

Object:

This project combines a button, an LED, and a temperature sensor. The LED will blink based on the temperature reading. If the button is pressed, the system will read the temperature and adjust the LED's blinking speed based on the temperature.

Programming Fundamentals name

- *Variables and Data Types*: Variables are used to define the GPIO pin numbers for the LED, button, and temperature sensor.
- *int*: Used to store GPIO pin numbers and the raw sensor data.
- *Lists*: Used to store temperature readings for calculating an average if needed.
- *Math Functions and Data Type Conversions*: Used to convert raw ADC sensor data into temperature in Celsius.
- *Control Structures (if-else, while)*:
  - *if-else*: To control the LED's blinking speed based on temperature and the button's state.
  - *while*: Used to monitor the button and temperature sensor continuously.

Use Syntax

- *Pin(pin_number, Pin.OUT)*: Defines the GPIO pin for the LED as an output.
- *Pin(pin_number, Pin.IN, Pin.PULL_UP)*: Defines the GPIO pin for the button as an input with a pull-up resistor.
- *ADC(Pin(pin_number))*: Defines the GPIO pin for reading the analog temperature sensor.
- *if condition:*: Used to adjust LED blinking speed based on the temperature.
- *while condition:*: Creates a loop for continuous temperature monitoring and button interaction.

Requirement component:

- ESP32 or ESP8266
- LED
- Button
- Temperature sensor (e.g., LM35 or TMP36)
- Resistors (220Ω for LED, 10kΩ for button if using external pull-up resistor)
- Breadboard
- Jumper wires

Circuit diagram:

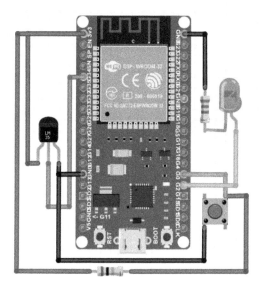

Circuit connection:

- Connect the LED's positive leg (anode) to GPIO 2 through a 220Ω resistor, and connect the negative leg (cathode) to GND.
- Connect one side of the button to GPIO 0, and the other side to GND. Use a 10kΩ pull-up resistor between GPIO 0 and 3.3V (if not using an internal pull-up).
- Connect the temperature sensor's VCC to 3.3V, GND to GND, and the analog output to an ADC pin (e.g., GPIO 34 on ESP32).

Micropython code

```python
from machine import ADC, Pin
import time

led_pin = 2         # Define LED GPIO pin
button_pin = 0      # Define button GPIO pin
sensor_pin = 34     # Define temperature sensor pin (int)

led = Pin(led_pin, Pin.OUT)
button = Pin(button_pin, Pin.IN, Pin.PULL_UP)
sensor = ADC(Pin(sensor_pin))  # Initialize ADC for temperature sensor

# Configure ADC width (optional, depends on your ESP32 variant)
sensor.atten(ADC.ATTN_11DB)    # Full-scale voltage (3.3V)
```

```python
def read_temperature():
    raw_value = sensor.read()
    voltage = (raw_value / 4095) * 3.3   # Convert raw value to voltage
(ESP32 12-bit ADC)
    temperature = voltage * 100          # For LM35 sensor: 10mV = 1°C
    return temperature

while True:
    if button.value() == 0:   # Button pressed (active low)
        temperature = read_temperature()

        if temperature > 30:   # If temperature is above 30°C
            blink_delay = 0.1   # Fast blink
        else:
            blink_delay = 0.5   # Slow blink

        for _ in range(5):   # Blink 5 times
            led.on()
            time.sleep(blink_delay)
            led.off()
            time.sleep(blink_delay)

        time.sleep(0.1)   # Debounce delay for button reading
```

Code Explanation

- *led_pin, button_pin, sensor_pin*: Defines the GPIO pins for the LED, button, and temperature sensor using the *int* data type.
- *read_temperature()*: Reads the raw ADC value from the temperature sensor, converts it to voltage, and then converts it to temperature in Celsius (for an LM35 sensor).
- *if button.value()* == *0*: Checks if the button is pressed.
- *if temperature > 30*: Adjusts the LED blinking speed based on the temperature. The LED blinks faster if the temperature is above 30°C.
- *for _ in range(5)*: Blinks the LED 5 times at the specified speed based on the temperature.
- *time.sleep(0.1)*: Introduces a debounce delay to avoid multiple readings when the button is pressed.

Note:

- You can adjust the temperature threshold and blinking speed based on your project requirements.
- The temperature sensor calibration (e.g., for LM35 or TMP36) can be adjusted by modifying the conversion formula in *read_temperature()*.

Project -2: Smart Fan Control Based on Temperature Sensor Using ESP32/ESP8266 and MicroPython

Object:

This project demonstrates how to control a fan (or motor) based on temperature readings using a temperature sensor and relay or transistor as an actuator. When the temperature exceeds a defined threshold, the fan will automatically turn on, and when the temperature drops below the threshold, the fan will turn off.

Programming Fundamentals name

- *Variables and Data Types*: Variables are used to define GPIO pin numbers, temperature thresholds, and sensor readings.
- *int*: Used for GPIO pin numbers and temperature threshold.
- *Math Functions and Data Type Conversions*: Used to convert raw ADC data from the temperature sensor into Celsius.
- *Control Structures (if-else, while)*:
  - *if-else*: Controls the fan's state based on temperature readings.
  - *while*: Continuously monitors the temperature to control the fan.

Use Syntax

- *Pin(pin_number, Pin.OUT)*: Defines the GPIO pin for the fan relay or transistor as an output.
- *Pin(pin_number, Pin.IN, Pin.PULL_UP)*: Defines the GPIO pin for the button as an input (optional for manual override).
- *ADC(Pin(pin_number))*: Reads the analog value from the temperature sensor.
- *if condition:*: Checks if the temperature exceeds the threshold to control the fan.
- *while condition:*: Monitors temperature continuously for automatic fan control.

Requirement component:

- ESP32 or ESP8266
- Temperature sensor (e.g., LM35 or TMP36)
- Fan or DC motor (connected via relay or NPN transistor)
- Relay module or NPN transistor (for fan control)
- Diode (if using a transistor to prevent back EMF)
- Breadboard
- Jumper wires

Circuit diagram:

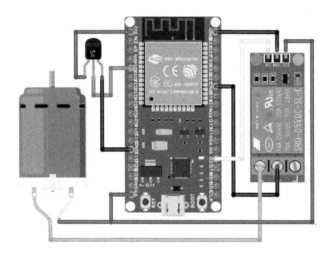

Circuit connection:

- Connect the temperature sensor's VCC to 3.3V, GND to GND, and the analog output to an ADC pin (e.g., GPIO 34 on ESP32).
- Connect the fan's positive terminal to an external 5V/12V power supply, and connect the negative terminal to the relay's NO (Normally Open) pin or the transistor's collector.
- Connect the relay/transistor control pin to a GPIO pin (e.g., GPIO 2).
- Optionally, connect a button to GPIO 0 for manual fan control.

Micropython code

```python
from machine import ADC, Pin
import time

fan_pin = 2          # GPIO for fan control (relay or transistor)
sensor_pin = 34      # GPIO for temperature sensor (ADC)
threshold_temp = 30  # Temperature threshold in Celsius
fan = Pin(fan_pin, Pin.OUT)
sensor = ADC(Pin(sensor_pin))   # Initialize ADC for temperature sensor
sensor.atten(ADC.ATTN_11DB)     # Set ADC attenuation for full range (0
to 3.3V)

def read_temperature():
    raw_value = sensor.read()
    voltage = (raw_value / 4095) * 3.3  # Convert raw ADC value to
voltage (12-bit ADC)
    temperature = voltage * 100          # For LM35 sensor: 10mV = 1°C
    return temperature

while True:
    temperature = read_temperature()
    print("Current Temperature:", temperature)

    if temperature >= threshold_temp:   # Turn on fan if temp exceeds
threshold
        fan.on()
        print("Fan ON")
    else:
        fan.off()
        print("Fan OFF")

    time.sleep(1)  # Delay before next reading
```

Code Explanation

- *fan_pin, sensor_pin*: These variables define the GPIO pins for the fan and temperature sensor.
- *threshold_temp = 30*: Sets the temperature threshold to 30°C, above which the fan turns on.
- *read_temperature()*: Converts the raw ADC value from the sensor into a temperature reading in Celsius.
- *if temperature >= threshold_temp*: Checks if the temperature exceeds the defined threshold and controls the fan accordingly.
- *fan.on()* and *fan.off()*: These commands control the fan's state via the relay or transistor.

Note:

- Adjust the temperature threshold as needed for your project.
- Make sure the relay or transistor is rated for the fan or motor you are controlling.

Project-3: Automated Light Control Based on Ambient Light Sensor Using ESP32/ESP8266 and MicroPython

Object:
This project automates the control of a light (LED or relay for a larger light) based on readings from an ambient light sensor. When the light level drops below a certain threshold, the light will automatically turn on, and it will turn off when the ambient light level increases.

Programming Fundamentals name
- *Variables and Data Types*: Variables are used to define GPIO pin numbers, light thresholds, and sensor data.
- *int*: Used for GPIO pin numbers and the light level threshold.
- *Math Functions and Data Type Conversions*: Converts raw ADC values from the light sensor into meaningful light levels.
- *Control Structures (if-else, while)*:
  - *if-else*: Controls the light's state based on the ambient light sensor readings.
  - *while*: Used to continuously monitor light levels and control the light.

Use Syntax
- *Pin(pin_number, Pin.OUT)*: Defines the GPIO pin for the LED or relay as an output.
- *ADC(Pin(pin_number))*: Reads the analog value from the ambient light sensor.
- *if condition:*: Checks if the light level is below the threshold to control the light.
- *while condition:*: Continuously monitors ambient light levels for automatic control.

Requirement component:
- ESP32 or ESP8266
- Ambient light sensor (e.g., LDR or BH1750)
- LED or a light bulb connected via a relay
- Resistors (220Ω for LED, optional resistor for LDR)
- Relay module (for controlling larger lights)

Circuit diagram:

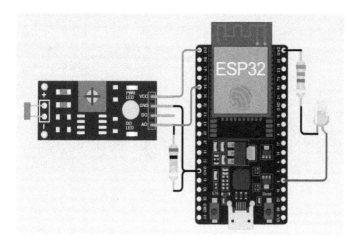

Circuit connection:
- Connect the LDR sensor between 3.3V and an ADC pin (e.g., GPIO 34 on ESP32), with a pull-down resistor (10kΩ) connected to GND.
- Connect the LED's positive leg (anode) to GPIO 2 through a 220Ω resistor and the negative leg (cathode) to GND.
- Alternatively, for a relay, connect the relay's input pin to GPIO 2, the common pin to the light's power supply, and the normally open pin to the light's positive terminal.

Micropython code

```python
from machine import ADC, Pin
import time

# GPIO pin definitions
led_pin = 2  # GPIO for LED or relay control
sensor_pin = 34  # GPIO for light sensor (ADC)
threshold_light = 1000  # Light level threshold (adjust based on sensor)

# Initialize pins
light = Pin(led_pin, Pin.OUT)  # LED or relay output pin
sensor = ADC(Pin(sensor_pin))  # Initialize ADC for light sensor

# Set attenuation for the sensor (to read 0-3.3V range)
sensor.atten(ADC.ATTN_11DB)  # Configure ADC for a wider voltage range
(up to 3.6V)
sensor.width(ADC.WIDTH_12BIT)  # Set ADC resolution to 12-bit (0-4095)

# Function to read light level
```

```
def read_light_level():
    raw_value = sensor.read()  # Read raw ADC value
    light_level = (raw_value / 4095) * 100  # Convert ADC value to
percentage (0-100%)
    return light_level

# Main loop
while True:
    light_level = read_light_level()  # Get the light level
    print("Ambient Light Level:", light_level)

    # Control the light based on the threshold
    if light_level < threshold_light:  # If light level is below the
threshold
        light.on()  # Turn on the LED or relay
        print("Light ON")
    else:
        light.off()  # Turn off the LED or relay
        print("Light OFF")

    time.sleep(1)  # Delay before the next reading
```

Code Explanation

- *led_pin, sensor_pin*: Defines GPIO pins for the light and ambient light sensor.
- *threshold_light = 1000*: Sets the light threshold, below which the light will turn on.
- *read_light_level()*: Reads the raw ADC value from the light sensor and converts it to a percentage to represent ambient light.
- *if light_level < threshold_light*: Checks if the ambient light is below the threshold and controls the light accordingly.
- *light.on()* and *light.off()*: These commands control the light or relay based on the sensor readings.

Note:

- Adjust the light threshold based on the sensor used and your project's requirements.
- If you are using a relay, ensure that it is rated for the light or appliance being controlled.
- You can replace the LED with a larger light connected through the relay for real-world applications like home lighting automation.

Pulse Width Modulation (PWM)

Project-1: Light-Dependent LED Brightness Control Using PWM with ESP32/ESP8266 and MicroPython

Object:
This project demonstrates how to use Pulse Width Modulation (PWM) to control the brightness of an LED based on input from a light sensor. The brightness of the LED will adjust dynamically based on the ambient light level.

Programming Fundamentals name
- *Control Structures*: The *if-else* and *while* loops are used to control the LED brightness and adjust PWM based on sensor readings.
- *Functions*: Used to encapsulate PWM adjustments and sensor reading in reusable code blocks.
- *Variables*: Used to store GPIO pin numbers, sensor readings, and PWM duty cycles for dynamic control.

Use Syntax
- *PWM(Pin(pin_number), freq=frequency)*: Initializes a GPIO pin for PWM output with a specified frequency.
- *pwm.duty(duty_cycle)*: Adjusts the PWM duty cycle to control brightness or motor speed (range is 0-1023 for ESP8266, 0-65535 for ESP32).
- *ADC(Pin(pin_number))*: Reads analog data from a sensor.
- *if condition:*: Used to adjust brightness or motor speed based on sensor input.
- *while condition:*: Continuously monitors sensor input and dynamically adjusts the PWM signal.

Requirement component:
- ESP32 or ESP8266
- LED
- Light sensor (e.g., LDR or BH1750)
- Resistors (220Ω for LED, optional resistor for LDR)
- Breadboard
- Jumper wires

Circuit diagram:

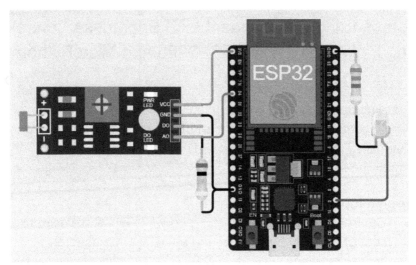

Circuit connection:

- Connect the LED's positive leg (anode) to GPIO 2 through a 220Ω resistor, and connect the negative leg (cathode) to GND.
- Connect the light sensor (LDR) between 3.3V and an ADC pin (e.g., GPIO 34 for ESP32), with a pull-down resistor (10kΩ) connected to GND.

Micropython code

```
from machine import Pin, PWM, ADC
import time
led_pin = 2 # GPIO for LED
sensor_pin = 34 # GPIO for light sensor (ADC)

led = PWM(Pin(led_pin), freq=1000) # Initialize PWM for LED with 1kHz
frequency
sensor = ADC(Pin(sensor_pin)) # Initialize ADC for light sensor

def read_light_level():
    raw_value = sensor.read()
    light_level = (raw_value / 4095) * 100 # Convert ADC value to
percentage
    return light_level
def adjust_led_brightness():
    light_level = read_light_level()
    duty_cycle = int((100 - light_level) * 1023 / 100) # Convert light
level to PWM duty cycle
    led.duty(duty_cycle) # Adjust LED brightness based on light level
while True:
    adjust_led_brightness()
    time.sleep(0.1) # Small delay for smooth adjustments
```

Code Explanation

- *led_pin, sensor_pin*: Define the GPIO pins for the LED and light sensor.
- *PWM(Pin(led_pin), freq=1000)*: Initializes PWM on the LED pin with a frequency of 1kHz.
- *sensor = ADC(Pin(sensor_pin))*: Initializes the ADC to read analog values from the light sensor.
- *read_light_level()*: Reads the ADC value from the light sensor and converts it to a percentage (0-100).
- *adjust_led_brightness()*: Dynamically adjusts the LED brightness based on the ambient light level by converting the light level to a PWM duty cycle.
- *while True*: Continuously adjusts the LED brightness in real-time based on the light sensor readings.

Note:

- Adjust the pull-down resistor and threshold for the light sensor as needed, depending on the specific LDR or light sensor used.
- You can easily modify this code to control other devices, like motors, based on sensor input by adjusting the PWM signal accordingly.

Project -2: Controlling a Servo Motor Based on Light Sensor Input

Object:

This project demonstrates how to control the position of a servo motor using PWM signals based on input from a light sensor. The servo will adjust its angle based on the amount of ambient light detected.

Programming Fundamentals name

- *Control Structures*: The *if-else* and *while* loops are used to control the servo's position based on light sensor readings.
- *Functions*: Encapsulate sensor reading and PWM adjustments in reusable blocks to dynamically control the servo motor.
- *Variables*: Used to store GPIO pin numbers, sensor readings, and PWM duty cycles for adjusting the servo motor's position.

Use Syntax

- *PWM(Pin(pin_number), freq=frequency)*: Initializes a GPIO pin for PWM output to control the servo.
- *pwm.duty_u16(duty_cycle)*: Adjusts the PWM duty cycle to control the servo's angle (for ESP32).
- *pwm.duty(duty_cycle)*: Used for adjusting duty cycle in ESP8266 (range is 0-1023).
- *ADC(Pin(pin_number))*: Reads analog data from the light sensor.
- *if condition:*: Used to adjust the servo motor's position based on the light sensor input.
- *while condition:*: Continuously monitors sensor input and dynamically adjusts the servo motor's position.

Requirement component:

- ESP32 or ESP8266
- Servo motor (e.g., SG90)
- Light sensor (e.g., LDR or BH1750)
- Resistors (10kΩ for LDR)
- External power supply (5V for the servo motor)
- Breadboard
- Jumper wires

Circuit diagram:

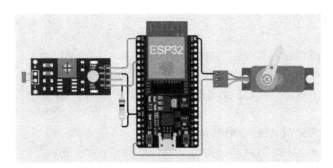

Circuit connection:

- Connect the LDR sensor between 3.3V and an ADC pin (e.g., GPIO 34 for ESP32), with a pull-down resistor (10kΩ) connected to GND.
- Connect the servo motor's signal wire to GPIO 2 (for PWM control), the power wire to 5V, and the ground wire to GND on the ESP32/ESP8266.

Micropython code

```
from machine import Pin, PWM, ADC
import time
servo_pin = 2 # GPIO for controlling the servo
sensor_pin = 34 # GPIO for light sensor (ADC)

servo = PWM(Pin(servo_pin), freq=50) # Initialize PWM for servo motor
with 50Hz frequency
sensor = ADC(Pin(sensor_pin)) # Initialize ADC for light sensor

def read_light_level():
    raw_value = sensor.read()
    light_level = (raw_value / 4095) * 100 # Convert ADC value to
percentage (0-100)
    return light_level
def adjust_servo_angle():
    light_level = read_light_level()
    duty_cycle = int((light_level / 100) * 102) + 40 # Convert light
level to PWM duty cycle (0-180 degrees for SG90 servo)
    servo.duty(duty_cycle) # Adjust servo position based on light level
while True:
    adjust_servo_angle()
    time.sleep(0.1) # Small delay for smooth adjustments
```

Code Explanation

- *servo_pin, sensor_pin*: Defines GPIO pins for the servo motor and light sensor.
- *PWM(Pin(servo_pin), freq=50)*: Initializes PWM on the servo pin with a frequency of 50Hz, which is standard for controlling servos.
- *sensor = ADC(Pin(sensor_pin))*: Initializes the ADC to read analog values from the light sensor.
- *read_light_level()*: Reads the ADC value from the light sensor and converts it into a percentage.
- *adjust_servo_angle()*: Adjusts the servo motor's angle by converting the light level into a PWM duty cycle that corresponds to servo positions (between 0 and 180 degrees).
- *while True*: Continuously adjusts the servo motor's position in real-time based on the light sensor readings.

Note:

- The PWM duty cycle for controlling the servo motor is mapped between 40 and 142 (approximately 0 to 180 degrees). Adjust the duty cycle range as needed for your specific servo motor.

Project -3: Temperature-Controlled Servo Motor Using ESP32/ESP8266 and MicroPython

Object:
This project controls a servo motor based on the input from a temperature sensor. The servo's angle changes according to the temperature reading. This can be used in applications like automated ventilation systems or temperature-based mechanical adjustments.

Programming Fundamentals name
- *Control Structures*: The *if-else* and *while* loops are used to control the servo's position based on temperature sensor readings.
- *Functions*: Encapsulate sensor reading and PWM adjustments in reusable blocks for dynamic control of the servo motor.
- *Variables*: Used to store GPIO pin numbers, sensor readings, and PWM duty cycles to adjust the servo motor's angle.

Use Syntax
- *PWM(Pin(pin_number), freq=frequency)*: Initializes a GPIO pin for PWM output to control the servo.
- *pwm.duty_u16(duty_cycle)*: Adjusts the PWM duty cycle to control the servo's angle (for ESP32).
- *pwm.duty(duty_cycle)*: Used for adjusting duty cycle in ESP8266 (range is 0-1023).
- *ADC(Pin(pin_number))*: Reads analog data from the temperature sensor.
- *if condition:*: Used to adjust the servo motor's position based on the temperature sensor input.
- *while condition:*: Continuously monitors the temperature and dynamically adjusts the servo motor's position.

Requirement component:
- ESP32 or ESP8266
- Servo motor (e.g., SG90)
- Temperature sensor (e.g., LM35 or TMP36)
- Resistors (optional depending on the sensor)

Circuit diagram:

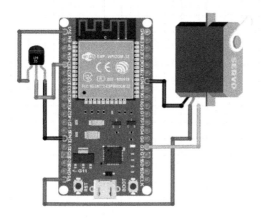

Circuit connection:

- Connect the temperature sensor's VCC to 3.3V, GND to GND, and the output pin to an ADC pin (e.g., GPIO 34 for ESP32).
- Connect the servo motor's signal wire to GPIO 2 (for PWM control), the power wire to 5V, and the ground wire to GND on the ESP32/ESP8266.

Micropython code

```
from machine import Pin, PWM, ADC
import time
servo_pin = 2 # GPIO for controlling the servo
sensor_pin = 34 # GPIO for temperature sensor (ADC)
servo = PWM(Pin(servo_pin), freq=50) # Initialize PWM for servo motor
at 50Hz
sensor = ADC(Pin(sensor_pin)) # Initialize ADC for temperature sensor
def read_temperature():
    raw_value = sensor.read()
    voltage = (raw_value / 4095) * 3.3 # Convert raw ADC value to
voltage
    temperature = voltage * 100 # For LM35 sensor, 10mV = 1 degree
Celsius
    return temperature
def adjust_servo_angle():
    temperature = read_temperature()
    duty_cycle = int((temperature / 50) * 102) + 40 # Map temperature
(0-50°C) to PWM duty cycle (0-180 degrees)
    servo.duty(duty_cycle) # Adjust servo position based on temperature
while True:
    adjust_servo_angle()
    time.sleep(1) # Small delay for smooth adjustments
```

Code Explanation

- *servo_pin, sensor_pin*: Defines GPIO pins for the servo motor and temperature sensor.
- *PWM(Pin(servo_pin), freq=50)*: Initializes PWM on the servo pin with a frequency of 50Hz, which is required for controlling servos.
- *sensor = ADC(Pin(sensor_pin))*: Initializes the ADC to read analog values from the temperature sensor.
- *read_temperature()*: Converts the raw ADC value from the temperature sensor into a temperature reading in Celsius.
- *adjust_servo_angle()*: Adjusts the servo motor's angle by mapping the temperature range (0-50°C) to a PWM duty cycle corresponding to the servo's position (0 to 180 degrees).
- *while True*: Continuously adjusts the servo motor's position in real-time based on the temperature sensor readings.

Note:

- Adjust the temperature range and duty cycle mapping as needed for your application. The example above maps temperatures from 0°C to 50°C to servo positions between 0 and 180 degrees.
- Make sure the servo motor is powered by a suitable external power supply (typically 5V for an SG90 servo).
- This project can be modified to control other mechanical systems that need to respond to temperature changes, such as automated fans or blinds.

Communication Protocols

Project-1: Temperature and Humidity-Based Servo Control

Object:

This project demonstrates how to control a servo motor based on temperature and humidity readings from a DHT22 sensor using PWM. The servo's angle is dynamically adjusted based on the temperature or humidity, depending on the application. This can be useful for smart climate control systems, such as opening vents or windows based on environmental conditions.

Programming Fundamentals name

- *Control Structures*: The *if-else* and *while* loops are used to control the servo motor based on temperature and humidity readings from the DHT22 sensor.
- *Functions*: Used to encapsulate sensor reading and PWM control of the servo motor.
- *Variables*: Used to store GPIO pin numbers, sensor readings, and PWM duty cycles for servo control.
- *Communication Protocols*: The DHT22 sensor communicates using a single-wire protocol to transmit temperature and humidity data.

Use Syntax

- *PWM(Pin(pin_number), freq=frequency)*: Initializes a GPIO pin for PWM output to control the servo.
- *pwm.duty_u16(duty_cycle)*: Adjusts the PWM duty cycle to control the servo's angle (for ESP32).
- *dht.DHT22(Pin(pin_number))*: Initializes the DHT22 sensor to read temperature and humidity.
- *if condition:*: Used to control the servo motor based on the sensor input.
- *while condition:*: Continuously monitors sensor data and adjusts the servo position accordingly.

Requirement component:

- ESP32 or ESP8266
- Servo motor (e.g., SG90)
- DHT22 sensor

Circuit diagram:

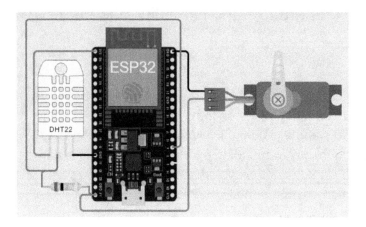

Circuit connection:
- Connect the DHT22 sensor's VCC to 3.3V, GND to GND, and the data pin to GPIO 4 on the ESP32/ESP8266 (with a 10kΩ pull-up resistor between VCC and data pin).
- Connect the servo motor's signal wire to GPIO 2, the power wire to 5V, and the ground wire to GND.

Micropython code

```
from machine import Pin, PWM import dht import time
servo_pin = 2 # GPIO for controlling the servo
sensor_pin = 4 # GPIO for DHT22 sensor
servo = PWM(Pin(servo_pin), freq=50) # Initialize PWM for servo motor
at 50Hz
dht_sensor = dht.DHT22(Pin(sensor_pin)) # Initialize DHT22 sensor
def read_temperature_humidity():
dht_sensor.measure()
temperature = dht_sensor.temperature()
humidity = dht_sensor.humidity()
return temperature, humidity
def adjust_servo_based_on_temp():
temperature, _ = read_temperature_humidity()
duty_cycle = int((temperature / 50) * 102) + 40 # Map temperature (0-
50°C) to PWM duty cycle
servo.duty(duty_cycle) # Adjust servo position based on temperature
def adjust_servo_based_on_humidity():
_, humidity = read_temperature_humidity()
duty_cycle = int((humidity / 100) * 102) + 40 # Map humidity (0-100%)
to PWM duty cycle
servo.duty(duty_cycle) # Adjust servo position based on humidity
while True:
adjust_servo_based_on_temp() # or use adjust_servo_based_on_humidity()
for humidity control
time.sleep(2) # Delay between sensor readings
```

Code Explanation

- *servo_pin, sensor_pin*: Define GPIO pins for the servo motor and the DHT22 sensor.
- *PWM(Pin(servo_pin), freq=50)*: Initializes PWM on the servo pin with a frequency of 50Hz, which is required for controlling servos.
- *dht.DHT22(Pin(sensor_pin))*: Initializes the DHT22 sensor to read temperature and humidity.
- *read_temperature_humidity()*: Reads the temperature and humidity data from the DHT22 sensor using the single-wire communication protocol.
- *adjust_servo_based_on_temp()*: Adjusts the servo motor's position by mapping the temperature range (0-50°C) to a PWM duty cycle for servo control.
- *adjust_servo_based_on_humidity()*: Adjusts the servo motor's position based on humidity, mapping the humidity range (0-100%) to the servo's PWM duty cycle.
- *while True*: Continuously adjusts the servo motor's position in real-time based on temperature or humidity readings from the DHT22 sensor.

Note:

- You can choose whether to control the servo based on temperature or humidity by calling either *adjust_servo_based_on_temp()* or *adjust_servo_based_on_humidity()* in the loop.
- Ensure the DHT22 sensor is properly powered and connected with a pull-up resistor on the data line for reliable communication.
- Adjust the temperature and humidity ranges as needed based on the environmental conditions you want to monitor.

Project-2: Designing a Multi-Sensor Monitoring System

Object:
This project demonstrates how to create a multi-sensor monitoring system that integrates various sensors (such as temperature, humidity, light, and distance sensors) to monitor environmental conditions. The system will display the sensor data on an OLED screen or send it to a cloud platform for remote monitoring.

Programming Fundamentals name
- *Control Structures*: The *if-else* and *while* loops manage data collection from each sensor and trigger alerts or actions based on the sensor readings.
- *Functions*: Encapsulate sensor reading and data handling in reusable blocks.
- *Variables*: Store GPIO pin numbers, sensor readings, and thresholds for each sensor.
- *Communication Protocols*: Integrate multiple sensors using I2C (for OLED display), 1-wire (for DHT22), and analog inputs (for sensors like LDR and distance sensors).

Use Syntax
- *ADC(Pin(pin_number))*: Reads analog data from sensors like light or distance sensors.
- *dht.DHT22(Pin(pin_number))*: Initializes the DHT22 sensor for reading temperature and humidity data.
- *i2c = I2C(scl=Pin(scl_pin), sda=Pin(sda_pin))*: Initializes I2C for communication with the OLED display.
- *if condition:*: Used to check if the sensor values cross a defined threshold to trigger actions.
- *while condition:*: Continuously monitors sensor data for real-time updates.

Requirement component:
- ESP32 or ESP8266
- DHT22 (Temperature and Humidity Sensor)
- LDR (Light Sensor)
- Ultrasonic Sensor (e.g., HC-SR04 for distance measurement)

- OLED display (I2C interface)
- Resistors (for LDR, pull-up resistor for DHT22)
- Breadboard
- Jumper wires

Circuit connection:
- Connect the DHT22 sensor's VCC to 3.3V, GND to GND, and the data pin to GPIO 4 on the ESP32/ESP8266 (with a 10kΩ pull-up resistor between VCC and data pin).
- Connect the LDR between 3.3V and an ADC pin (e.g., GPIO 34), with a 10kΩ pull-down resistor to GND.
- Connect the ultrasonic sensor's VCC to 5V, GND to GND, trigger pin to GPIO 2, and echo pin to GPIO 5.
- Connect the OLED display's SDA pin to GPIO 21 and SCL pin to GPIO 22 for I2C communication.

Micropython code

```python
from machine import Pin, ADC, I2C
import dht
import ssd1306  # For OLED display
import time

# Sensor and display setup
dht_sensor = dht.DHT22(Pin(4))  # DHT22 on GPIO 4
ldr = ADC(Pin(34))  # LDR on GPIO 34
trigger = Pin(2, Pin.OUT)  # Trigger for ultrasonic sensor
echo = Pin(5, Pin.IN)  # Echo for ultrasonic sensor
i2c = I2C(scl=Pin(22), sda=Pin(21))  # I2C for OLED display
oled = ssd1306.SSD1306_I2C(128, 64, i2c)  # Initialize OLED

# Function to read LDR value
def read_light_level():
    raw_value = ldr.read()
    light_level = (raw_value / 4095) * 100  # Convert ADC value to
percentage
    return light_level

# Function to read DHT22 temperature and humidity
def read_dht22():
    dht_sensor.measure()
    temperature = dht_sensor.temperature()
    humidity = dht_sensor.humidity()
    return temperature, humidity

# Function to measure distance with ultrasonic sensor
def measure_distance():
    trigger.off()
    time.sleep_us(2)
    trigger.on()
    time.sleep_us(10)
```

```python
    trigger.off()

    while echo.value() == 0:
        signaloff = time.ticks_us()
    while echo.value() == 1:
        signalon = time.ticks_us()

    timepassed = signalon - signaloff
    distance = (timepassed * 0.0343) / 2  # Calculate distance in cm
    return distance

# Function to update OLED display
def update_display(temp, humidity, light, distance):
    oled.fill(0)  # Clear screen
    oled.text("Temp: {} C".format(temp), 0, 0)
    oled.text("Humidity: {} %".format(humidity), 0, 10)
    oled.text("Light: {} %".format(light), 0, 20)
    oled.text("Distance: {} cm".format(distance), 0, 30)
    oled.show()
# Main loop
while True:
    temperature, humidity = read_dht22()
    light_level = read_light_level()
    distance = measure_distance()

    update_display(temperature, humidity, light_level, distance)
    time.sleep(2)  # Update every 2 seconds
```

Code Explanation

- *DHT22 Sensor (dht.DHT22)*: Used to measure temperature and humidity.
- *LDR (ADC)*: Reads analog data from the light sensor and converts it into a percentage (0-100%).
- *Ultrasonic Sensor (measure_distance)*: Sends a pulse and measures the echo to calculate distance in centimeters.
- *OLED Display (ssd1306)*: Updates the screen with current sensor readings (temperature, humidity, light level, and distance).
- *while True*: Continuously reads data from all sensors and updates the OLED display every 2 seconds.

Note:

- Ensure the correct wiring for the I2C OLED display, with the appropriate SDA and SCL pins on the ESP32/ESP8266.
- You can modify this code to include more sensors or actions, such as sending data to a cloud platform (e.g., via MQTT or HTTP).

Part 3 : Get started with IOT with Micropython

Chapter 13. Networking Wifi

In this chapter, you'll learn how to connect the ESP32 or ESP8266 to a Wi-Fi network, manage connections, and monitor the network status using MicroPython. We'll cover the basic setup using *WiFi.begin()*, how to disconnect from a network, and how to display the connection status and IP address. Understanding these concepts is crucial for developing IoT applications where devices need to communicate over the internet or local networks.

Syntax Table

Topic	Syntax	Simple Example
Connecting to Wi-Fi	*WiFi.begin(ssid, password)*	*WiFi.begin("MyNetworkSSID", "MyNetworkPassword")*
Disconnecting from Wi-Fi	*WiFi.disconnect( )*	*WiFi.disconnect()*
Get IP Address (Station Mode)	*station.ifconfig()[0]*	*print("Device IP:", station.ifconfig()[0])*
Check if Connected	*station.isconnect ed()*	*if station.isconnected(): print("Connected")*

1. Basic Wi-Fi Setup

Connecting ESP32/ESP8266 to Wi-Fi using WiFi.begin()

What is

WiFi.begin(ssid, password) is a function used to connect an ESP32 or ESP8266 microcontroller to a Wi-Fi network by providing the network's SSID (name) and password. This function is part of the ESP WiFi library, used in MicroPython or Arduino programming, and helps establish internet connectivity for your project.

Why is Important?

Connecting to a Wi-Fi network is crucial for IoT (Internet of Things) projects where the ESP32 or ESP8266 devices need to communicate over the internet, collect data from sensors, send data to a server, or interact with cloud services. The *WiFi.begin()* function is the starting point for enabling such connectivity.

Syntax

```
WiFi.begin(ssid, password)
```

Syntax Explanation

- *ssid*: The name of the Wi-Fi network to connect to (must be a string).
- *password*: The password for the Wi-Fi network (must be a string).

Code Example

```
WiFi.begin("MyNetworkSSID", "MyNetworkPassword")
```

Notes

- The WiFi.begin() function initiates the connection process, but the connection is not instantaneous. You may need to wait until the connection is successful by repeatedly checking the connection status.
- ESP32 and ESP8266 may need different Wi-Fi library imports depending on the platform being used.

Warnings

- Ensure that the SSID and password are correct; otherwise, the connection will fail.

Disconnecting ESP32/ESP8266 from Wi-Fi using WiFi.disconnect() in Arduino and MicroPython

What is

`WiFi.disconnect()` is a function used to disconnect the ESP32 or ESP8266 microcontroller from the currently connected Wi-Fi network. It can be used in both Arduino and MicroPython environments to stop the ongoing Wi-Fi connection.

Why is Important?

Disconnecting from a Wi-Fi network can be important for power management, security reasons, or when switching between different networks. In certain IoT scenarios, it's also useful to disconnect after data transmission to save power or minimize exposure to unwanted networks.

Syntax

```
WiFi.disconnect()
```

Syntax Explanation

This function does not take any arguments and, when called, it disconnects the device from the current Wi-Fi network.

Code Example

```
WiFi.disconnect()
```

Notes

- After calling `WiFi.disconnect()`, the device will no longer be connected to any Wi-Fi network, and any ongoing communication requiring the internet will be interrupted.
- This is often used when you need to perform a task locally and do not require Wi-Fi for an extended period.

Warnings

- Make sure that disconnecting from the network is safe in the context of your application, especially if you rely on a continuous connection for critical functions.
- If your device needs to reconnect later, you will need to call `WiFi.begin()` again with the correct credentials.

Project : ESP32 Wi-Fi Connection: Connect to Home Wi-Fi and Display Connection Status on Serial Monitor

Object

To connect the ESP32 to a home Wi-Fi network and display the connection status (e.g., connecting, success, failure) on the serial monitor using MicroPython.

Programming Fundamentals name

- *network.WLAN(network.STA_IF)* - Used to set up the ESP32 in Station mode to connect to an existing Wi-Fi network.
- *station.connect(ssid, password)* - Initiates a connection to the specified Wi-Fi network.
- *station.isconnected()* - Checks if the ESP32 has successfully connected to the Wi-Fi network.
- *print()* - Displays the messages and connection status on the serial monitor for feedback.

Use Syntax

```
network.WLAN(network.STA_IF)
station.connect(ssid, password)
station.isconnected()
print("message")
```

Requirement component

- ESP32 or ESP8266 module
- USB cable for connecting the ESP32 to a computer
- Computer with MicroPython IDE (such as Thonny IDE)
- Wi-Fi network credentials (SSID and password)

Circuit diagram

Since this project is about connecting to Wi-Fi, no additional components are required. The ESP32/ESP8266 should be connected to the computer via a USB cable for programming.

Circuit connection

- Connect the ESP32/ESP8266 to your computer using a USB cable.
- Ensure that the MicroPython firmware is installed on the ESP32 and the correct serial port is selected in the IDE (e.g., Thonny).

Micropython code

```
import network import time
ssid = "YourNetworkSSID" password = "YourNetworkPassword"
station = network.WLAN(network.STA_IF)
station.active(True)
station.connect(ssid, password)
print("Connecting to Wi-Fi...")
while not station.isconnected():
    time.sleep(1)
if station.isconnected():
    print("Connected successfully to Wi-Fi")
    print("Device IP Address:", station.ifconfig()[0])
else:
    print("Failed to connect to Wi-Fi")
```

Replace Wi-Fi Credentials:

- Replace *"YourNetworkSSID"* and *"YourNetworkPassword"* with your actual Wi-Fi details.

Save and Run the Code:

- Save the file with a .py extension, such as *wifi_connect.py*.
- Click the "Run" button in Thonny to upload and execute the code on the ESP32.

Check Output:

The console in Thonny will show messages like:

Connecting to Wi-Fi...

Connected successfully to Wi-Fi

Device IP Address: 192.168.x.x

If the connection fails, it will print:

Failed to connect to Wi-Fi

Reasult

```
>>> %Run -c $EDITOR_CONTENT

  MPY: soft reboot
  Connecting to Wi-Fi...
  Connected successfully to Wi-Fi
  Device IP Address: 192.168.1.107
```

Note

- Make sure the Wi-Fi credentials are correct for successful connection.
- The ESP32 must be in the range of your Wi-Fi router for stable connectivity.
- If the connection fails, double-check the Wi-Fi credentials and the network's availability.
- This basic structure is suitable for beginners to understand how to connect the ESP32 to Wi-Fi, with step-by-step logic included for better understanding.

2. Connection Status & IP Information

Getting the IP Address of ESP32 Using WiFi.localIP() in MicroPython

What is

WiFi.localIP() is a function used to retrieve the local IP address assigned to the ESP32 or ESP8266 microcontroller when it successfully connects to a Wi-Fi network. This IP address is used for communication within the local network.

Why is Important?

The IP address is essential for identifying the ESP32 or ESP8266 on the local network. It allows you to communicate with the device, for example, when accessing a web server hosted on the ESP32 or sending data between devices. Knowing the IP address is crucial for debugging network issues and for establishing reliable device communication.

Syntax

```
WiFi.localIP()
```

Syntax Explanation

This function does not take any arguments. It returns the local IP address of the ESP32/ESP8266 as a string.

Code Example

```
ip_address = WiFi.localIP()
print("Device IP Address:", ip_address)
```

Notes
- The IP address returned by *WiFi.localIP()* is only valid when the ESP32 or ESP8266 is connected to a Wi-Fi network.
- You can use this IP address to connect to the ESP32 from other devices on the same network, such as accessing a web server or sending data.

Warnings
- If the device is not connected to a Wi-Fi network, calling *WiFi.localIP()* may return an empty or invalid IP address.
- Make sure to check the connection status using *WiFi.isconnected()* before attempting to use *WiFi.localIP()*.

Getting the IP Address of ESP32 in Access Point Mode Using WiFi.softAPIP() in MicroPython

What is
WiFi.softAPIP() is a function used to retrieve the IP address of the ESP32 or ESP8266 when it is in Access Point (AP) mode. In this mode, the ESP32 acts as a Wi-Fi network that other devices can connect to, rather than connecting to an existing network.

Why is Important?
In Access Point mode, the ESP32 creates its own Wi-Fi network, allowing other devices to connect directly to it. The IP address returned by *WiFi.softAPIP()* is crucial for interacting with the ESP32 while it acts as an AP, such as accessing web servers hosted on the device or facilitating communication between the ESP32 and connected clients.

Syntax

```
WiFi.softAPIP()
```

Syntax Explanation
This function does not take any arguments. It returns the IP address of the ESP32/ESP8266 in Access Point mode as a string.

Code Example

```
ap_ip_address = WiFi.softAPIP()
print("Access Point IP Address:", ap_ip_address)
```

Notes
- The default IP address for ESP32 in Access Point mode is often *192.168.4.1*, but this can be changed through configuration.
- *WiFi.softAPIP()* is only relevant when the ESP32 is set up as an AP. In Station mode, use *WiFi.localIP()* instead.

Warnings
- Ensure that the ESP32 is correctly configured in Access Point mode before calling *WiFi.softAPIP()*; otherwise, the function may not return a valid IP address.
- Devices connected to the ESP32 AP will have their own IP addresses within the subnet managed by the ESP32.

Project Display ESP32 IP Address: Displaying the IP Address After Connecting to Wi-Fi

Object
To connect the ESP32 to a Wi-Fi network and then display the device's IP address on either an external screen or the serial monitor using MicroPython.

Programming Fundamentals name
- *WiFi.begin(ssid, password)* - Used to connect the ESP32 to the Wi-Fi network.
- *WiFi.localIP()* - Used to retrieve the IP address assigned to the ESP32 once connected to the network.
- *print("message")* - Used to display text and the IP address on the serial monitor.

Use Syntax
```
WiFi.begin(ssid, password)
WiFi.localIP()
print("Device IP Address:", WiFi.localIP())
```

Requirement component
- ESP32 or ESP8266 module
- USB cable for programming
- Computer with MicroPython IDE (like Thonny)
- Wi-Fi network credentials (SSID and password)

Circuit connection

- Connect the ESP32/ESP8266 to the computer using a USB cable.
- Ensure that the correct serial port is selected in the IDE for code upload and serial monitoring.

Micropython code

```
import network import time
ssid = "YourNetworkSSID" password = "YourNetworkPassword"
station = network.WLAN(network.STA_IF)
station.active(True)
station.connect(ssid, password)
while not station.isconnected():
    print("Connecting to Wi-Fi...")
    time.sleep(1)
print("Connected successfully")
print("Device IP Address:", station.ifconfig()[0])
```

Replace Wi-Fi Credentials:

- Replace *"YourNetworkSSID"* and *"YourNetworkPassword"* with your actual Wi-Fi details.

Save and Run the Code:

- Save the file with a .py extension, such as *wifi_connect.py*.
- Click the "Run" button in Thonny to upload and execute the code on the ESP32.

Check Output:

The console in Thonny will show messages like:

Connecting to Wi-Fi...

Connected successfully to Wi-Fi

Device IP Address: 192.168.x.x

If the connection fails, it will print:

Failed to connect to Wi-Fi

Reasult

```
>>> %Run -c $EDITOR_CONTENT

 MPY: soft reboot
 Connecting to Wi-Fi...
 Connected successfully to Wi-Fi
 Device IP Address: 192.168.1.107
```

Note

- Ensure the Wi-Fi credentials are correct, and the Wi-Fi network is active for successful connectivity.

3. Wi-Fi Mode Selection

Setting ESP32 to Station Mode Using WiFi.mode(WIFI_STA)

What is
WiFi.mode(WIFI_STA) is a function used to set the ESP32 in "Station" (STA) mode, which means it will connect to an existing Wi-Fi network, similar to how a smartphone or laptop connects to a router. This mode is ideal for when the ESP32 needs to act as a client device in an IoT application.

Why is Important?
Setting the ESP32 to Station mode is important because it allows the device to connect to a Wi-Fi network and communicate with other devices over the internet or a local network. Station mode is essential for applications where the ESP32 needs to send or receive data from servers or interact with other connected devices in the network.

Syntax

```
WiFi.mode(WIFI_STA)
```

Syntax Explanation
WIFI_STA: A predefined constant that represents Station mode. This tells the ESP32 to act as a client and connect to an available Wi-Fi network.

Code Example
```
import network station = network.WLAN(network.STA_IF)
station.active(True)
station.mode(WIFI_STA)
```

Notes
- Station mode is one of the modes supported by the ESP32, with others being Access Point (AP) mode and both Station and AP mode simultaneously.
- In most IoT applications, the ESP32 is set to Station mode to connect to a Wi-Fi router.

Warnings
- Make sure to activate the interface using *station.active(True)* before setting the mode.

Setting ESP32 to Access Point Mode Using WiFi.mode(WIFI_AP)

What is
WiFi.mode(WIFI_AP) is a function used to set the ESP32 in "Access Point" (AP) mode, which allows the device to create its own Wi-Fi network. In this mode, other devices can connect to the ESP32 as if it were a Wi-Fi hotspot.

Why is Important?
Setting the ESP32 to Access Point mode is important when you want to create a local network that other devices can connect to directly. This is useful for creating a local server, managing configurations, or creating an isolated network for peer-to-peer communication without requiring an existing router.

Syntax

```
WiFi.mode(WIFI_AP)
```

Syntax Explanation
WIFI_AP: A predefined constant that represents Access Point mode. This sets the ESP32 to act as a Wi-Fi network that other devices can join.

Code Example

```
import network ap = network.WLAN(network.AP_IF)
ap.active(True)
ap.mode(WIFI_AP)
```

Notes
- Access Point mode is useful for creating a private network without needing an external router.
- You can configure the SSID, password, and other settings of the access point after activating it.

Warnings
- In Access Point mode, the ESP32 cannot connect to another Wi-Fi network while it is serving as a hotspot unless it is also configured in Station mode (dual mode).
- Ensure security settings are correctly configured to avoid unauthorized access to your ESP32 in AP mode.

Enabling Both Station and Access Point Modes Using WiFi.mode(WIFI_AP_STA)

What is

WiFi.mode(WIFI_AP_STA) is a function used to set the ESP32 to operate in both "Station" (STA) mode and "Access Point" (AP) mode simultaneously. This allows the ESP32 to connect to an existing Wi-Fi network as a client while also creating its own Wi-Fi network for other devices to join.

Why is Important?

Enabling both Station and Access Point modes is important when the ESP32 needs to connect to an external network for internet access while allowing other devices to connect directly to it. This can be useful for device configuration, local communication, or sharing data between the ESP32 and multiple clients without disconnecting from the main network.

Syntax

```
WiFi.mode(WIFI_AP_STA)
```

Syntax Explanation

WIFI_AP_STA: A predefined constant that enables both Station and Access Point modes simultaneously. This allows the ESP32 to act as both a client and a Wi-Fi hotspot.

Code Example

```
import network wifi = network.WLAN(network.STA_IF)
wifi.active(True)
wifi.mode(WIFI_AP_STA)
```

Notes

- Using both modes at the same time gives flexibility, as the ESP32 can connect to an existing Wi-Fi network while also allowing direct connections from other devices.
- This mode is useful for IoT applications where the device needs to send data to the cloud while allowing local control via a connected smartphone or computer.

Warnings

- Operating in both modes simultaneously may use more power and require more system resources, which can impact performance.

Project Dual Mode ESP32: Connect to Wi-Fi as a Client (Station) and Create a Hotspot (AP) for Other Devices with Indicator LED

Object
To configure the ESP32 to connect to an existing Wi-Fi network as a client while simultaneously creating a Wi-Fi hotspot for other devices to connect to, using MicroPython, and to use an indicator LED to show the connection status.

Programming Fundamentals name
- *network.WLAN(network.STA_IF)* - Used to set up the ESP32 in Station mode to connect to an existing Wi-Fi network.
- *network.WLAN(network.AP_IF)* - Used to set up the ESP32 in Access Point mode to create a Wi-Fi network for other devices.
- *WiFi.mode(WIFI_AP_STA)* - Used to enable both Station and Access Point modes at the same time.
- *machine.Pin()* - Used to configure the GPIO pins for input/output (e.g., to control an LED).
- *print()* - Used to display messages and statuses on the serial monitor.

Use Syntax

```
network.WLAN(network.STA_IF)
network.WLAN(network.AP_IF)
WiFi.mode(WIFI_AP_STA)
machine.Pin(pin_number, mode)
print("message")
```

Requirement component
- ESP32 or ESP8266 module
- USB cable for programming
- Computer with MicroPython IDE (such as Thonny IDE)
- Wi-Fi network credentials (SSID and password)
- LED
- Resistor (220 ohms)
- Jumper wires
- Breadboard

Circuit diagram

- Connect an LED to the ESP32's GPIO pin (e.g., GPIO 2).
- Connect a 220-ohm resistor in series with the LED to limit the current.
- Connect the anode of the LED to GPIO 2 (or any suitable pin).
- Connect the cathode of the LED to GND.

Circuit connection

- Connect the ESP32/ESP8266 to the computer using a USB cable.
- Connect the LED to GPIO 2 through a resistor, and connect the other end to GND.
- Ensure that the MicroPython firmware is installed on the ESP32 and the correct serial port is selected in the IDE (e.g., Thonny).

Micropython code

```python
import network import time import machine
# Set up the LED indicator on GPIO 2
led = machine.Pin(2, machine.Pin.OUT)
# Set up Station mode (STA) to connect to an existing Wi-Fi network
ssid = "YourNetworkSSID"
password = "YourNetworkPassword"
station = network.WLAN(network.STA_IF)
station.active(True)
station.connect(ssid, password)
print("Connecting to Wi-Fi as a client...")
led.value(1) # Turn on LED to indicate connection in progress
while not station.isconnected():
    time.sleep(1)
if station.isconnected():
    print("Connected successfully to Wi-Fi")
    print("Device IP Address:", station.ifconfig()[0])
    led.value(0) # Turn off LED to indicate successful connection
else:
    print("Failed to connect to Wi-Fi")
    led.value(1) # Keep LED on to indicate failure
# Set up Access Point (AP) mode to create a hotspot
ap = network.WLAN(network.AP_IF)
ap.active(True)
ap.config(essid="ESP32_Hotspot", password="HotspotPassword")
print("Access Point created")
print("AP IP Address:", ap.ifconfig()[0])
```

Replace Wi-Fi Credentials:

- Replace *"YourNetworkSSID"* and *"YourNetworkPassword"* with your actual Wi-Fi network's SSID and password.
- Set the desired name (*"ESP32_Hotspot"*) and password for the ESP32's Access Point (hotspot) mode.

Save and Run the Code:

- Save the file with a .py extension (e.g., *wifi_ap_connect.py*).
- Click "Run" in Thonny or your chosen IDE to upload and execute the code on your ESP32.

Check Output:

In the Thonny console or terminal, you should see something like:

```
Connecting to Wi-Fi as a client...
Connected successfully to Wi-Fi
Device IP Address: 192.168.x.x
Access Point created
AP IP Address: 192.168.4.1
```

If the connection to Wi-Fi fails, the message will say:

```
Failed to connect to Wi-Fi
```

LED Indicator:

- The LED connected to GPIO 2 will turn *on* while the ESP32 is attempting to connect to Wi-Fi.
- If the connection is successful, the LED will turn *off*.
- If the ESP32 fails to connect to Wi-Fi, the LED will stay *on* as an indicator of failure.

Note

- The LED serves as a visual indicator of the connection status: it is on while connecting and off when connected.
- The ESP32 can operate in both Station and Access Point modes simultaneously, which is useful for maintaining a connection to an external network while also providing a local hotspot.
- Make sure to secure both networks with passwords to avoid unauthorized access.
- Double-check your GPIO pin connections and LED polarity to ensure proper functionality.

4. Network Scanning

Scanning for Nearby Wi-Fi Networks Using WiFi.scanNetworks()

What is

WiFi.scanNetworks() is a function used to scan for nearby Wi-Fi networks. It returns a list of available Wi-Fi networks, including information like the SSID (network name), signal strength, and security type.

Why is Important?

Scanning for available Wi-Fi networks is crucial in applications where the ESP32 needs to dynamically select a network, provide a user with available options, or automatically connect to the strongest or preferred network. It is especially useful for setting up Wi-Fi connections in new environments where the available networks may not be known beforehand.

Syntax

```
WiFi.scanNetworks()
```

Syntax Explanation

This function does not take any arguments. It returns a list of tuples, where each tuple represents a detected network, containing information like the SSID, RSSI (signal strength), and security type.

Code Example

```
import network station = network.WLAN(network.STA_IF)
station.active(True)
networks = station.scan()
for network in networks:
    print("SSID:", network[0], "| Signal Strength:", network[3])
```

Notes

- The *WiFi.scanNetworks()* function is typically used in Station mode to find nearby networks.
- The results include details such as SSID (name), BSSID (MAC address), channel, RSSI (signal strength), and encryption type.

Warnings

- Scanning for networks may consume a significant amount of power, so use it sparingly in battery-powered applications.

Getting the SSID of the i-th Network Using WiFi.SSID(i)

What is
WiFi.SSID(i) is a function used to retrieve the SSID (name) of the i-th Wi-Fi network found during a scan. It allows you to access specific network information from a list of available networks.

Why is Important?
Getting the SSID of a scanned network is important for providing users with a list of available Wi-Fi networks to connect to. It is essential in applications where the ESP32 needs to present network options for selection or automate the connection process to a known network.

Syntax

```
WiFi.SSID(i)
```

Syntax Explanation
i The index of the scanned network for which you want to retrieve the SSID. The index *i* must be a valid integer representing a scanned network.

Code Example

```
import network station = network.WLAN(network.STA_IF)
station.active(True)
networks = station.scan()
for i in range(len(networks)):
    print("Network", i, "SSID:", networks[i][0])
```

Notes
- The index *i* is zero-based, meaning the first network is accessed using *i = 0*, the second network with *i = 1*, and so on.
- The SSID is the public name of a Wi-Fi network, which can help identify the networks that the ESP32 can connect to.

Warnings
- Ensure that the index *i* is within the range of available networks, or an error may occur.
- The scan results may change if the networks are unstable or if scanning occurs repeatedly, so always check the number of networks found before accessing an index.

Project: Wi-Fi Network Scanner: Scan for Available Wi-Fi Networks and Display SSIDs and Signal Strengths

Object
To program the ESP32 to scan for nearby Wi-Fi networks and display the SSIDs and signal strengths on the serial monitor using MicroPython.

Programming Fundamentals name
- *network.WLAN(network.STA_IF)* - Used to set the ESP32 in Station mode, which is required for scanning nearby networks.
- *station.scan()* - Used to scan for available Wi-Fi networks and gather information like SSID and RSSI.
- *print()* - Used to display the scanned network information on the serial monitor.

Use Syntax

```
network.WLAN(network.STA_IF)
station.scan()
print("message")
```

Requirement component
- ESP32 or ESP8266 module
- USB cable for programming
- Computer with MicroPython IDE (such as Thonny IDE)

Circuit diagram
This project involves scanning for Wi-Fi networks, so no additional hardware components are necessary. The ESP32/ESP8266 is connected to the computer via USB for programming and monitoring.

Circuit connection

- Connect the ESP32/ESP8266 to the computer using a USB cable.
- Ensure that the MicroPython firmware is installed on the ESP32 and the correct serial port is selected in the IDE (e.g., Thonny).

Micropython code

```python
import network import time
# Set up Station mode to scan for available networks
station = network.WLAN(network.STA_IF)
station.active(True)
print("Scanning for available Wi-Fi networks...")
networks = station.scan()
# Display the SSID and RSSI of each network found
for i, network in enumerate(networks):
    ssid = network[0].decode('utf-8')
    rssi = network[3]
    print(f"Network {i + 1}: SSID: {ssid}, Signal Strength (RSSI):
{rssi} dBm")
```

Replace Wi-Fi Credentials:

- No Wi-Fi credentials are needed in this script, as the code is designed to scan and display available networks. Simply run the code as is.

Save and Run the Code:

- Save the file with a .py extension (for example, *wifi_scan.py*).
- Open Thonny or your preferred IDE and click "Run" to execute the code on your ESP32.

Check Output:

In the console, you should see the available Wi-Fi networks along with their SSIDs and signal strengths (RSSI values), like this:

Scanning for available Wi-Fi networks...
Network 1: SSID: YourWiFi, Signal Strength (RSSI):
-45 dBm
Network 2: SSID: AnotherWiFi, Signal Strength
(RSSI): -70 dBm

```
>>> %Run -c $EDITOR_CONTENT
MPY: soft reboot
Scanning for available Wi-Fi networks...
Network 1: SSID: H, Signal Strength (RSSI): -35 dBm
Network 2: SSID: Soha, Signal Strength (RSSI): -91 dBm
Network 3: SSID: RPI Hostel 3, Signal Strength (RSSI): -92 dBm
Network 4: SSID: , Signal Strength (RSSI): -92 dBm
Network 5: SSID: Principal House main , Signal Strength (RSSI): -95 dBm
```

Note

- The *network[0]* value represents the SSID, which is in bytes and needs to be decoded to display it properly.
- The RSSI (signal strength) is typically a negative value, with values closer to zero indicating a stronger signal.

5. Event Handling

Registering a Function to Handle Wi-Fi Events Using WiFi.onEvent(WiFiEvent)

What is
WiFi.onEvent(WiFiEvent) is a function used to register a callback function that handles Wi-Fi-related events, such as connection, disconnection, and IP address changes. It allows you to react to specific Wi-Fi status changes automatically.

Why is Important?
Handling Wi-Fi events is important to create robust applications where you need to monitor the connection status dynamically and take actions based on specific events. For example, reconnecting automatically if disconnected, or logging messages when the ESP32 connects to or disconnects from the network. It helps to enhance reliability and user experience.

Syntax

```
WiFi.onEvent(WiFiEvent)
```

Syntax Explanation
WiFiEvent: A callback function that you define to handle specific Wi-Fi events. This function will be called automatically when certain Wi-Fi events occur.

Code Example

```
import network import time
def wifi_event_handler(event):
    if event == network.EVENT_STAMODE_CONNECTED:
        print("Wi-Fi connected")
    elif event == network.EVENT_STAMODE_DISCONNECTED:
        print("Wi-Fi disconnected")
station = network.WLAN(network.STA_IF)
station.active(True)
station.on_event(wifi_event_handler)
station.connect("YourNetworkSSID", "YourNetworkPassword")
```

Notes
- You need to register the event handler before starting the Wi-Fi connection process to ensure all events are captured.
- You can handle various events, such as *EVENT_STAMODE_CONNECTED*, *EVENT_STAMODE_DISCONNECTED*, and more, depending on your requirements.

Warnings
- Make sure the callback function is defined properly and handles different events gracefully to avoid unexpected behavior.
- Incorrect handling of Wi-Fi events may lead to infinite loops or unrecoverable errors, especially if the connection repeatedly fails.

Project: Wi-Fi Connection Status Logger: Log and Display Wi-Fi Connection or Disconnection Events Using WiFi.onEvent()

Object
To set up the ESP32 to automatically log and display events related to Wi-Fi connection or disconnection, using the *WiFi.onEvent()* function with MicroPython. The goal is to make the ESP32 capable of responding to changes in Wi-Fi status.

Programming Fundamentals name
- *network.WLAN(network.STA_IF)* - Used to set the ESP32 in Station mode to connect to an existing Wi-Fi network.
- *WiFi.onEvent()* - Used to register a callback function that handles Wi-Fi-related events, such as connection and disconnection.
- *print()* - Used to display messages about Wi-Fi events on the serial monitor for debugging and monitoring.

Use Syntax

```
network.WLAN(network.STA_IF)
WiFi.onEvent(WiFiEvent)
print("message")
```

Requirement component

- ESP32 or ESP8266 module
- USB cable for programming
- Computer with MicroPython IDE (such as Thonny IDE)
- Wi-Fi network credentials (SSID and password)

Circuit diagram

This project involves logging Wi-Fi events, so no additional hardware components are necessary. The ESP32/ESP8266 should be connected to the computer via USB for programming and monitoring.

Circuit connection

- Connect the ESP32/ESP8266 to the computer using a USB cable.
- Ensure that the MicroPython firmware is installed on the ESP32 and the correct serial port is selected in the IDE (e.g., Thonny).

Micropython code

```python
import network import time
# Define a callback function to handle Wi-Fi events
def wifi_event_handler(event):
    if event == network.EVENT_STAMODE_CONNECTED:
        print("Wi-Fi connected successfully")
    elif event == network.EVENT_STAMODE_DISCONNECTED:
        print("Wi-Fi disconnected")
# Set up Station mode to connect to an existing Wi-Fi network
station = network.WLAN(network.STA_IF)
station.active(True)
# Register the Wi-Fi event handler
station.on_event(wifi_event_handler)
# Start the connection process
station.connect("YourNetworkSSID", "YourNetworkPassword")
# Wait for the connection to establish
while not station.isconnected():
    print("Attempting to connect...")
    time.sleep(1)
print("Connected to Wi-Fi with IP:", station.ifconfig()[0])
```

Replace Wi-Fi Credentials:

Replace *"YourNetworkSSID"* and *"YourNetworkPassword"* with your actual Wi-Fi network's SSID and password in the following line:

```python
station.connect("YourNetworkSSID",
"YourNetworkPassword")
```

Save and Run the Code:
- Save the file with a `.py` extension (for example, *wifi_event_handler.py*).
- Open Thonny or your preferred IDE, then click "Run" to execute the code on your ESP32

Check Output:
The console will display messages indicating the connection status, like:

```
Attempting to connect...
Wi-Fi connected successfully
Connected to Wi-Fi with IP: 192.168.x.x
```

If the connection is lost, you'll see:

```
Wi-Fi disconnected
```

Note
- Registering a callback function using *WiFi.onEvent()* allows for automated handling of Wi-Fi connection events without needing to poll for status changes constantly.
- The connection and disconnection events provide real-time feedback that can be helpful in debugging connectivity issues.
- Make sure the SSID and password are correct for a successful connection. If the network connection fails, the event handler will log the event appropriately.

6. Advanced Network Management

Setting a Static IP Address Using WiFi.config(ip, gateway, subnet)

What is
WiFi.config(ip, gateway, subnet) is a function used to set a static IP address, gateway, and subnet mask for the ESP32 or ESP8266 when it connects to a Wi-Fi network. This is used instead of relying on DHCP to automatically assign an IP address.

Why is Important?

Setting a static IP address is important when you need the ESP32 to always use the same IP address within your network, such as when it needs to be accessed by other devices, like a server or for remote control purposes. Static IP addresses provide reliability and stability, especially in applications where the ESP32 needs to communicate with other devices consistently without the risk of a changing IP address.

Syntax

```
WiFi.config(ip, gateway, subnet)
```

Syntax Explanation

- *ip*: The static IP address to assign to the ESP32, provided as a string (e.g., "192.168.1.50").
- *gateway*: The gateway IP address, usually the IP address of the router, also provided as a string (e.g., "192.168.1.1").
- *subnet*: The subnet mask, provided as a string (e.g., "255.255.255.0").

Code Example

```
import network
station = network.WLAN(network.STA_IF)
station.active(True)
station.config(ip="192.168.1.50", gateway="192.168.1.1",
subnet="255.255.255.0")
station.connect("YourNetworkSSID", "YourNetworkPassword")
while not station.isconnected():
    pass
print("Connected with Static IP:", station.ifconfig()[0])
```

Notes

- Ensure that the static IP address you assign is within the range of the network and is not already in use by another device.
- Setting a static IP is useful for applications where the device needs to be accessed frequently and predictably, such as a web server hosted on the ESP32.

Warnings

- If the IP address is incorrectly configured (e.g., conflicts with another device), the ESP32 may not be able to connect to the network properly.
- Make sure the gateway and subnet mask values are correct to avoid routing and connectivity issues within your network.

Setting a Custom Hostname Using WiFi.setHostname(name)

What is
WiFi.setHostname(name) is a function used to set a custom hostname for the ESP32. The hostname is the network name of the device, making it easier to identify when connected to a network.

Why is Important?
Setting a custom hostname is important because it allows you to easily identify the ESP32 on your network. Instead of seeing a generic name or an IP address, you can give the ESP32 a descriptive name, making it more convenient for management and troubleshooting, especially in networks with multiple devices.

Syntax

```
WiFi.setHostname(name)
```

Syntax Explanation
name: The desired hostname for the ESP32, provided as a string (e.g., "ESP32_Logger").

Code Example
```
import network
station = network.WLAN(network.STA_IF)
station.active(True)
station.config(dhcp_hostname="ESP32_Logger")
station.connect("YourNetworkSSID", "YourNetworkPassword")
while not station.isconnected():
    pass
print("Connected with Hostname:", "ESP32_Logger")
```

Notes
- The hostname can make it easier to access the ESP32 from other devices on the network, especially if you use the mDNS feature to access it via hostname.local.
- Hostnames must be unique within a network to prevent conflicts.

Warnings
- If the hostname is not set properly or conflicts with another device, it may lead to issues with network identification.
- The hostname setting may need to be configured before the ESP32 connects to the Wi-Fi network for it to take effect.

Adjusting Wi-Fi Transmission Power Using WiFi.setTxPower(power)

What is
WiFi.setTxPower(power) is a function used to adjust the Wi-Fi transmission power of the ESP32. The transmission power can be increased or decreased to control the range and power consumption of the Wi-Fi signal.

Why is Important?
Adjusting the transmission power is important in scenarios where you want to optimize the power consumption of the ESP32. Reducing power can help save battery life for battery-powered devices, while increasing power can improve the range in situations where a stronger signal is needed.

Syntax
```
WiFi.setTxPower(power)
```

Syntax Explanation
power: The desired transmission power level, usually set in dBm (e.g., 20 dBm for maximum power or 8 dBm for reduced power).

Code Example
```
import network
station = network.WLAN(network.STA_IF)
station.active(True)
station.connect("YourNetworkSSID", "YourNetworkPassword")
while not station.isconnected():
    pass
station.config(txpower=14) # Set transmission power to 14 dBm
print("Wi-Fi connected with adjusted transmission power.")
```

Notes
- Adjusting the power level affects both range and power consumption. High power increases range but also increases energy use.
- It is recommended to find a balance between transmission power and energy efficiency, depending on your use case.

Warnings
- Setting the transmission power too high may cause interference with other devices, especially in a congested Wi-Fi environment.

Disabling Wi-Fi Sleep Mode Using WiFi.setSleep(false)

What is
WiFi.setSleep(false) is a function used to disable the Wi-Fi sleep mode on the ESP32 or ESP8266. Disabling sleep mode ensures that the device maintains a continuous and uninterrupted connection to the Wi-Fi network, which can be useful for real-time applications.

Why is Important?
Disabling Wi-Fi sleep mode is important in applications where a stable, always-on connection is required, such as streaming data, real-time monitoring, or control applications. By keeping the connection active, you prevent latency or disconnections that may occur due to the power-saving features of sleep mode.

Syntax

```
WiFi.setSleep(false)
```

Syntax Explanation
false: Setting *false* will disable the Wi-Fi sleep mode, keeping the Wi-Fi module continuously active.

Code Example

```
import network
station = network.WLAN(network.STA_IF)
station.active(True)
station.config(ps_mode=network.WIFI_PS_NONE) # Disable sleep mode for
continuous connection
station.connect("YourNetworkSSID", "YourNetworkPassword")
while not station.isconnected():
    pass
print("Connected to Wi-Fi with sleep mode disabled.")
```

Notes

- Disabling sleep mode can improve connection reliability for tasks that require continuous data exchange.
- Sleep mode is typically enabled by default to save power, but it can introduce latency or momentary disconnections, which may not be suitable for some applications.

Warnings

- Disabling sleep mode will increase the power consumption of the ESP32/ESP8266, which may be a concern in battery-powered projects.
- Ensure that the power supply can handle the increased energy demands when sleep mode is disabled, especially for long-running applications.

Project Static IP Configuration and Power Management: Set a Static IP and Hostname for the ESP32 and Experiment with Power Management Settings

Object

To configure the ESP32 to use a static IP address, set a custom hostname, and experiment with power management settings using MicroPython to enhance stability, network accessibility, and optimize energy consumption.

Programming Fundamentals name

- *network.WLAN(network.STA_IF)* - Used to set the ESP32 in Station mode to connect to an existing Wi-Fi network.
- *station.config(ip, gateway, subnet)* - Used to configure a static IP address, gateway, and subnet mask, ensuring consistent identification on the network.
- *station.config(dhcp_hostname="hostname")* - Used to set a custom hostname, allowing easier identification of the ESP32 within the network.
- *station.config(ps_mode=network.WIFI_PS_NONE)* - Used to disable Wi-Fi sleep mode to maintain a stable and uninterrupted Wi-Fi connection.
- *print()* - Used to display network status information for debugging and monitoring purposes.

Use Syntax

```
network.WLAN(network.STA_IF)
station.config(ip="192.168.1.50", gateway="192.168.1.1",
subnet="255.255.255.0")
station.config(dhcp_hostname="ESP32_StaticDevice")
station.config(ps_mode=network.WIFI_PS_NONE)
print("message")
```

Requirement component
- ESP32 or ESP8266 module
- USB cable for programming
- Computer with MicroPython IDE (such as Thonny IDE)
- Wi-Fi network credentials (SSID and password)

Circuit diagram

This project involves configuring network settings and power management, so no additional hardware components are necessary. The ESP32/ESP8266 should be connected to the computer via USB for programming and monitoring.

Circuit connection
- Connect the ESP32/ESP8266 to the computer using a USB cable.
- Ensure that the MicroPython firmware is installed on the ESP32 and the correct serial port is selected in the IDE (e.g., Thonny).

Micropython code

```
import network import time
# Set up Station mode to connect to an existing Wi-Fi network
station = network.WLAN(network.STA_IF)
station.active(True)
# Set static IP, gateway, and subnet for the ESP32
station.config(ip="192.168.1.50", gateway="192.168.1.1",
subnet="255.255.255.0")
# Set a custom hostname for the ESP32
station.config(dhcp_hostname="ESP32_StaticDevice")
# Disable Wi-Fi sleep mode for a continuous connection
station.config(ps_mode=network.WIFI_PS_NONE)
# Connect to the Wi-Fi network
station.connect("YourNetworkSSID", "YourNetworkPassword")
# Wait for the connection to establish
while not station.isconnected():
    print("Attempting to connect...")
    time.sleep(1)
print("Connected to Wi-Fi with Static IP:", station.ifconfig()[0])
```

Replace Wi-Fi Credentials:

Replace *"YourNetworkSSID"* and *"YourNetworkPassword"* with your actual Wi-Fi network's SSID and password in the following line:

```
station.connect("YourNetworkSSID",
"YourNetworkPassword")
```

Save and Run the Code:

- Save the file with a `.py` extension (for example, *wifi_static_ip.py*).
- Open Thonny or your preferred IDE, and click "Run" to execute the code on your ESP32.

Check Output:

The console will display the connection status and the static IP address:

```
Attempting to connect...
Connected to Wi-Fi with Static IP: 192.168.1.50
```

Note

- Configuring a static IP ensures that the ESP32 is always accessible at the same IP address, which is useful for remote control or server applications.
- Disabling Wi-Fi sleep mode is recommended in applications requiring consistent data transmission, but it may lead to higher power consumption.

Common Mistakes and How to Avoid Them

1. **Incorrect SSID or Password**
   - **Mistake**: Entering the wrong SSID or password, leading to connection failure.
   - **How to Avoid**: Double-check the SSID and password to ensure they match your network credentials. *WiFi.begin("IncorrectSSID", "WrongPassword") – This will fail to connect.*
2. **Not Waiting for the Connection**
   - **Mistake**: Assuming the Wi-Fi connection is instantaneous and moving on without checking if it's established.
   - **How to Avoid**: Use a loop to wait until the device is connected before proceeding with network-related operations. *while not station.isconnected(): pass – Wait for connection to complete.*

Chapter-14 Building IoT Applications

1. Server Control Functions

ESP32 Web Server Functions: begin() and handleClient()

What is

begin() and *handleClient()* are functions typically used with the ESP32/ESP8266 web server libraries (such as ESPAsyncWebServer in Arduino) to initialize the web server and manage incoming client requests.

- *begin()*: This function is used to start the web server, making it ready to accept client connections.
- *handleClient()*: This function is used to continuously process incoming requests from clients and respond appropriately.

Why is Important?

- *begin()* is important because it initializes the web server, allowing it to start listening for connections. Without calling *begin()*, the server won't function.
- *handleClient()* is essential for handling requests from clients. It checks if a client has made a request and processes it, ensuring the web server can serve web pages or execute commands based on requests.

Syntax

```
server.begin()
server.handleClient()
```

Syntax Explanation

- *server.begin()*: This command starts the web server.
- *server.handleClient()*: This function is called in the main loop to process any client requests. Without calling this repeatedly, the server won't be able to respond to incoming HTTP requests.

Code Example

```
import network import socket import time
# Connect to Wi-Fi
station = network.WLAN(network.STA_IF)
station.active(True)
station.connect("YourNetworkSSID", "YourNetworkPassword")
while not station.isconnected():
    time.sleep(1)
print("Connected to Wi-Fi with IP:", station.ifconfig()[0])
# Create a simple web server
server = socket.socket()
server.bind(('', 80))
server.listen(5)
# Web server functions begin() and handleClient()
server.begin() # Start the server
while True:
    server.handleClient() # Handle incoming requests
```

Notes

- *begin()* must be called before the server can start accepting connections.
- *handleClient()* needs to be called regularly, usually inside a loop, to process any incoming HTTP requests from clients. Without this, the server won't respond.

Warnings

- Forgetting to call *server.begin()* will prevent the web server from running, and no clients will be able to connect.
- If *handleClient()* is not called frequently, client requests may not be processed, leading to delayed or missed responses. This is especially important in real-time applications.

Project: Basic Web Server: Setting Up a Web Server on ESP32/ESP8266 to Listen for and Handle Incoming HTTP Requests

Object

To set up a basic web server on an ESP32/ESP8266 that listens for incoming HTTP requests and responds with simple HTML content, using MicroPython. This project is aimed at beginners to help them understand how to make the ESP32 work as a web server.

Programming Fundamentals name

- *network.WLAN(network.STA_IF)* - Used to set up the ESP32 in Station mode, allowing it to connect to a Wi-Fi network. This lets the ESP32 communicate on your home Wi-Fi like your phone or computer.
- *socket.socket()* - Used to create a server socket that listens for incoming connections, enabling the ESP32 to act as a server.
- *server.bind(('', 80))* - Used to bind the server socket to a specific port (port 80 is used for web traffic).
- *server.listen(5)* - Used to make the server start listening for incoming connections from clients.
- *server.accept()* - Used to accept an incoming client connection and set up communication.
- *conn.recv(1024)* - Used to receive the incoming HTTP request from the client, allowing the ESP32 to understand what the client wants.
  conn.send(response) - Used to send the response (HTML content) back to the client.
- *conn.close()* - Used to close the connection with the client after sending the response.
- *print()* - Used to display messages about the connection and requests for debugging purposes.

Use Syntax

```
network.WLAN(network.STA_IF)
socket.socket()
server.bind(('', 80))
server.listen(5)
server.accept()
conn.recv(1024)
conn.send(response)
conn.close()
print("message")
```

Requirement component

- ESP32 or ESP8266 module
- USB cable for programming
- Computer with MicroPython IDE (such as Thonny IDE)
- Wi-Fi network credentials (SSID and password)

Circuit diagram

This project involves setting up a basic web server, so no additional hardware components are necessary. The ESP32/ESP8266 should be connected to the computer via USB for programming and monitoring.

Circuit connection

- Connect the ESP32/ESP8266 to the computer using a USB cable.
- Ensure that the MicroPython firmware is installed on the ESP32 and the correct serial port is selected in the IDE (e.g., Thonny).

Micropython code

```python
import network
import socket
import time
# Set up Station mode and connect to Wi-Fi
station = network.WLAN(network.STA_IF)
station.active(True)
station.connect("YourNetworkSSID", "YourNetworkPassword")
# Wait for the connection to establish
while not station.isconnected():
    print("Connecting to Wi-Fi...")
    time.sleep(1)
print("Connected to Wi-Fi with IP:", station.ifconfig()[0])

# Set up the server socket
server = socket.socket(socket.AF_INET, socket.SOCK_STREAM)
server.bind(('', 80))
server.listen(5)
print("Listening for incoming connections...")

# Handle incoming requests
while True:
    conn, addr = server.accept()
    print("Client connected from:", addr)
    request = conn.recv(1024)
    print("Request:", request)
    # Create a simple HTML response
    response = """HTTP/1.1 200 OK
Content-Type: text/html

<html>
    <body>
        <h1>Welcome to ESP32 Web Server!</h1>
    </body>
</html>
"""

    conn.send(response)
    conn.close()
```

Steps to Run the Code:

1. **Replace Wi-Fi Credentials:**

Replace `"YourNetworkSSID"` and `"YourNetworkPassword"` with your actual Wi-Fi network's SSID and password in the following line:

`station.connect("YourNetworkSSID", "YourNetworkPassword")`

2. **Save and Run the Code:**
    - Save the file with a `.py` extension (e.g., `wifi_web_server.py`).
    - Open Thonny or your preferred IDE, and click "Run" to upload and execute the code on your ESP32.

3. **Access the Web Server:**
    - Once the ESP32 connects to your Wi-Fi network, it will display its IP address.
    - Open a web browser and type the IP address of the ESP32 in the address bar (e.g., `http://192.168.x.x`).
    - You will see the message "Welcome to ESP32 Web Server!" displayed on the webpage.

← → C ⚠ Not secure 192.168.1.107

Welcome to ESP32 Web Server!

Note
- This basic web server setup is meant to introduce beginners to how the ESP32 can be used to serve web pages over a network.
- The IP address printed (`Connected to Wi-Fi with IP:`) is the one you can type into a web browser to access the ESP32's web server. For example, if it says `192.168.1.50`, you can type `http://192.168.1.50` in your browser to see the response.

2. Request Handling Functions

Setting up Web Routes Using on() and Handling 404 Errors Using onNotFound() on ESP32/ESP8266

What is
on() and *onNotFound()* are functions typically used in web server frameworks to define how the server should respond to specific URLs (routes) or handle requests when the requested page is not found (404 error).

- *on()*: This function is used to register a route (a specific URL path) and define how the server should respond when a client visits that path.
- *onNotFound()*: This function is used to handle requests for URLs that do not exist on the server, usually returning a "404 Not Found" error message or a custom error page.

Why is Important?
- *on()* is important because it allows the web server to handle different routes or URLs, making it more interactive and functional. For example, you can create routes like /status, /control, or /info and send different responses based on the path.
- *onNotFound()* is crucial for handling incorrect or non-existent URLs in a user-friendly way, such as showing a "404 Page Not Found" error instead of crashing the server.

Syntax
```
server.on(path, method, callback)
server.onNotFound(callback)
```

Syntax Explanation
- *server.on(path, method, callback)*: This registers a route at the URL *path* (e.g., /status), for a specific HTTP *method* (like GET or POST), and the *callback* function defines what the server will do when that route is requested.
- *server.onNotFound(callback)*: This sets the *callback* function that will be executed whenever a request is made to a non-existent path, typically displaying a "404 Not Found" page.

Code Example

```
import network import socket import time
# Set up Wi-Fi connection
station = network.WLAN(network.STA_IF)
station.active(True)
station.connect("YourNetworkSSID", "YourNetworkPassword")
while not station.isconnected():
    time.sleep(1)
print("Connected to Wi-Fi with IP:", station.ifconfig()[0])
# Set up the server
server = socket.socket()
server.bind(('', 80))
server.listen(5)
def handle_root():
    *return """HTTP/1.1 200 OK
Content-Type: text/html
<html><body><h1>Welcome to ESP32 Web Server</h1></body></html>"""*
def handle_404():
    *return """HTTP/1.1 404 Not Found
Content-Type: text/html
<html><body><h1>404 Page Not Found</h1></body></html>"""*
while True:
    conn, addr = server.accept()
    request = conn.recv(1024)
    if "/ " in request:
        response = handle_root()
    else:
        response = handle_404()
    conn.send(response)
    conn.close()
```

Notes

- In this example, the root URL (/) is handled by the *handle_root()* function, which sends back a simple HTML page.
- If the requested path is not /, the server responds with the *handle_404()* function, showing a custom "404 Not Found" page.

Warnings

- Make sure to define all necessary routes using *on()* or *onNotFound()* so that the server can handle every possible request.
- Failure to handle unknown routes with *onNotFound()* could lead to unpredictable behavior or errors when users request invalid URLs.

Project : LED Control via Web Interface: Controlling an LED Connected to ESP32 Using an HTML Button

Object
To create a web page that allows you to control an LED connected to the ESP32 by clicking an HTML button. This project is easy for beginners to understand how to create a simple web server and interact with hardware using MicroPython.

Programming Fundamentals name
- *machine.Pin()* - Sets up and controls the GPIO pins on the ESP32 to turn the LED on or off.
- *network.WLAN(network.STA_IF)* - Connects the ESP32 to your Wi-Fi network, enabling it to serve web pages.
- *socket.socket()* - Creates the server that allows other devices (like phones or computers) to connect to the ESP32.
- *conn.recv(1024)* - Receives the incoming request from the client, such as clicking the button on the web page.
- *conn.send(response)* - Sends the HTML content (web page) back to the client, allowing them to see changes in real-time.

Use Syntax
- *machine.Pin(LED_PIN, machine.Pin.OUT)* - Set up the LED pin as an output to control it.
- *network.WLAN(network.STA_IF)* - Set up the ESP32 to connect to your Wi-Fi as a client.
- *socket.socket()* - Create a new socket for communication.
- *conn.recv(1024)* - Receive up to 1024 bytes of data from the client.
- *conn.send(response)* - Send back a response (e.g., an HTML web page).

Requirement component
- ESP32 or ESP8266 module
- LED
- 220-ohm resistor
- Breadboard
- Jumper wires
- USB cable for programming
- Computer with MicroPython IDE (such as Thonny IDE)

Circuit diagram

1. Connect the longer leg of the LED (anode) to **GPIO 2** of the ESP32.
2. Connect the shorter leg of the LED (cathode) to one end of a 220-ohm resistor.
3. Connect the other end of the resistor to the **GND** pin of the ESP32.

Circuit connection

-   **GPIO 2** → LED anode (longer leg)

-   **GND** → Resistor → LED cathode (shorter leg)

-   Connect ESP32 to your computer using a USB cable.

Micropython code

```python
import network
import socket
import machine

# Set up the LED pin
led = machine.Pin(2, machine.Pin.OUT)

# Set up Wi-Fi connection
station = network.WLAN(network.STA_IF)
station.active(True)
station.connect("YourNetworkSSID", "YourNetworkPassword")

# Wait until connected to Wi-Fi
while not station.isconnected():
    print("Connecting to Wi-Fi...")

print("Connected to Wi-Fi with IP:", station.ifconfig()[0])

# Set up the server
server = socket.socket()
server.bind(('', 80))
server.listen(5)

# Function to create the web page
def web_page():
    if led.value() == 1:
        led_state = "ON"
    else:
        led_state = "OFF"

    html = """<html>
    <head><title>ESP32 LED Control</title></head>
    <body><h1>LED Control</h1>
    <p>LED is currently: <strong>""" + led_state + """</strong></p>
    <form action="/led_on"><button type="submit">Turn
ON</button></form>
```

```
    <form action="/led_off"><button type="submit">Turn
OFF</button></form>
    </body></html>"""
    return html

# Handle incoming requests
while True:
    conn, addr = server.accept()
    print("Client connected from:", addr)
    request = conn.recv(1024).decode()
    print("Request:", request)

    if "/led_on" in request:
        led.value(1)  # Turn LED ON
    if "/led_off" in request:
        led.value(0)  # Turn LED OFF

    response = web_page()
    conn.send("HTTP/1.1 200 OK\n")
    conn.send("Content-Type: text/html\n\n")
    conn.sendall(response)
    conn.close()
```

How to Save, Run, and Check Output:

Replace Wi-Fi Credentials: Update the following lines in the code with your Wi-Fi SSID and password:

```
ssid = "YourNetworkSSID"
password = "YourNetworkPassword"
```

1. **Upload the Code to ESP32:** Use an IDE like Thonny or another MicroPython-compatible tool to upload the code as `main.py` to your ESP32.
2. **Check the Output:**
   - Open a browser, enter the IP address printed in the console (e.g., `http://192.168.x.x`).
   - The web page will show the current state of the LED and allow you to turn it ON or OFF using the buttons.

ESP32 Web Server - LED Control

LED is currently: **OFF**

Turn ON

Turn OFF

Note

- Make sure to replace "YourNetworkSSID" and "YourNetworkPassword" with your actual Wi-Fi credentials.
- After the ESP32 connects to Wi-Fi, it will print an **IP address**. Use that IP address in your browser to access the web page (e.g., http://192.168.1.50).
- You can control the LED by clicking the **"Turn ON"** or **"Turn OFF"** buttons on the web page.

3. Response Functions

Sending HTTP Responses Using send(), sendHeader(), send_P() on ESP32/ESP8266

What is

send(), *sendHeader()*, and *send_P()* are functions used in web server programming to send HTTP responses to clients.

- *send()*: Sends the HTTP response to the client, including the status code, content type, and the body of the response.
- *sendHeader()*: Sends a specific HTTP header to the client, such as Content-Type, to provide additional information about the response.
- *send_P()*: Typically used to send data stored in program memory (e.g., HTML strings), useful for sending large or repeated content more efficiently.

Why is Important?

- *send()* is important because it is used to send the complete response to a client, including the HTML content of a web page.
- *sendHeader()* is crucial to set specific response headers, like content type (text/html) or caching instructions, allowing better control over how the response is handled by the browser.
- *send_P()* is used to optimize memory usage by sending content directly from program memory, helping save RAM on memory-limited devices like the ESP32/ESP8266.

Syntax

```
send(status_code, content, content_type)
sendHeader(header_name, header_value)
send_P(content, content_type)
```

Syntax Explanation

- *send(status_code, content, content_type)*: This sends a complete HTTP response with a specific status code (e.g., 200 for OK), the response body (e.g., HTML code), and the content type (e.g., text/html).
- *sendHeader(header_name, header_value)*: Sends a specific HTTP header, where *header_name* is the name of the header (e.g., Content-Type) and *header_value* is its value (e.g., text/html).
- *send_P(content, content_type)*: Sends the response content directly from program memory, which is useful for large or constant HTML content that should not be stored in RAM.

Code Example

```
import network
import socket
import machine
import time

# Set up the LED pin (GPIO2 on ESP32)
led = machine.Pin(2, machine.Pin.OUT)

# Replace with your Wi-Fi credentials
ssid = "H"
password = "1122334455667788999"

# Set up Wi-Fi connection
station = network.WLAN(network.STA_IF)
```

```python
station.active(True)
station.connect(ssid, password)

# Wait until connected to Wi-Fi
while not station.isconnected():
    print("Connecting to Wi-Fi...")
    time.sleep(1)

print("Connected to Wi-Fi with IP:", station.ifconfig()[0])

# Set up the web server
server = socket.socket(socket.AF_INET, socket.SOCK_STREAM)
server.bind(('', 80))  # Bind to port 80
server.listen(5)  # Listen for incoming connections

# Function to create the web page
def web_page():
    if led.value() == 1:
        led_state = "ON"
    else:
        led_state = "OFF"

    # Basic HTML structure for LED control
    html = """<html>
    <head><title>ESP32 LED Control</title></head>
    <body>
    <p>LED is currently: <strong>""" + led_state + """</strong></p>
    <form action="/led_on"><button type="submit">Turn
ON</button></form><br>
    <form action="/led_off"><button type="submit">Turn
OFF</button></form>
    </body></html>"""
    return html

# Handle incoming HTTP requests
while True:
    conn, addr = server.accept()  # Accept connection from client
    print("Client connected from:", addr)
    request = conn.recv(1024).decode()  # Get the request
    print("Request:", request)

    # Parse the request to toggle the LED state
    if "/led_on" in request:
        led.value(1)  # Turn LED ON
    if "/led_off" in request:
        led.value(0)  # Turn LED OFF

    # Send response to the client
    response = web_page()
    conn.send("HTTP/1.1 200 OK\n")
    conn.send("Content-Type: text/html\n\n")
    conn.sendall(response)
    conn.close()  # Close the connection
```

Upload the Code to ESP32:

- Connect your ESP32 to your computer via USB.
- Use an IDE like Thonny or another MicroPython-compatible tool.
- Set up Thonny for ESP32 by selecting `MicroPython` (`ESP32`) in the interpreter options.
- Paste the code into Thonny and save it as `main.py` on your ESP32.
- Click the "Run" button to execute the code.

Check the Output:

- Once the code runs, the console will display `Connected to Wi-Fi with IP: xxx.xxx.xxx.xxx`, showing the IP address assigned to the ESP32.
- Open a browser and enter the ESP32's IP address (e.g., `http://192.168.1.x`).
- You will see a web page showing the LED state and buttons to turn the LED ON or OFF.

Notes

- *send()* is used in MicroPython to send a complete response directly. It includes headers and HTML content, making it simple for beginners.
- The *sendHeader()* function can be used to send additional headers before sending the content if needed (e.g., for caching or content types).
- *send_P()* is not directly available in MicroPython, but similar functionality can be implemented by storing HTML in a variable and sending it.

Warnings

- If *send()* does not include the proper headers (like `Content-Type`), browsers may not interpret the response correctly.

- Using *sendHeader()* incorrectly or forgetting to send important headers may result in unexpected browser behavior, such as incorrect rendering of the response.
- Be careful with large content, as sending it directly from RAM (instead of using program memory) may exhaust the ESP32's limited resources.

Project: Temperature Monitoring Web Page: Display Temperature Sensor Readings on a Web Page Hosted by the ESP32

Object
To create a web page that displays real-time temperature readings from a sensor connected to the ESP32. This project uses MicroPython and aims to help beginners understand how to read sensor data and display it over a network using a web interface.

Programming Fundamentals name
- *machine.ADC()* - Used to read analog data from the temperature sensor connected to an ADC pin on the ESP32.
- *network.WLAN(network.STA_IF)* - Connects the ESP32 to a Wi-Fi network, allowing it to serve web pages.
- *socket.socket()* - Creates a server that listens for requests and allows devices to connect and retrieve temperature data.
- *time.sleep()* - Creates delays to control the frequency of updates, ensuring stable data readings.

Use Syntax
- *machine.ADC(PIN)* - Set up an analog pin to read data from the temperature sensor.
- *network.WLAN(network.STA_IF)* - Set up the ESP32 to connect to your Wi-Fi as a client.
- *socket.socket()* - Create a socket for communication to serve web pages.
- *time.sleep(1)* - Wait for a specified time (e.g., 1 second) to control the rate of data collection.

Requirement component
- ESP32 or ESP8266 module
- Temperature sensor (e.g., LM35 or DHT11)
- Breadboard
- Jumper wires
- USB cable for programming
- Computer with MicroPython IDE (such as Thonny IDE)

Circuit diagram

1. Connect the **VCC** of the temperature sensor to **3.3V** on the ESP32.
2. Connect the **GND** of the temperature sensor to **GND** on the ESP32.
3. Connect the **Data/Output** pin of the sensor to **GPIO 34** (or another ADC pin).

Circuit connection

- **VCC** → **3.3V** on ESP32

- **GND** → **GND** on ESP32

- **Data/Output** → **GPIO 34** (ADC pin) on ESP32

- Connect ESP32 to your computer using a USB cable.

Micropython code

```
import network
import socket
import machine
import time

# Set up the temperature sensor pin (assuming it's an analog sensor
like LM35)
sensor = machine.ADC(machine.Pin(34))  # Use GPIO 34 (analog input)
sensor.atten(machine.ADC.ATTN_11DB)  # Set attenuation to read the full
voltage range (0-3.3V)

# Replace with your Wi-Fi credentials
ssid = "H"
password = "1122334455667788999"

# Set up Wi-Fi connection
station = network.WLAN(network.STA_IF)
station.active(True)
station.connect(ssid, password)

# Wait until connected to Wi-Fi
while not station.isconnected():
    print("Connecting to Wi-Fi...")
    time.sleep(1)

print("Connected to Wi-Fi with IP:", station.ifconfig()[0])

# Set up the web server
server = socket.socket(socket.AF_INET, socket.SOCK_STREAM)
server.bind(('', 80))  # Bind to port 80
server.listen(5)  # Listen for incoming connections

# Function to create the web page displaying the temperature
def web_page():
```

```python
    # Get temperature reading (convert ADC value to temperature)
    adc_value = sensor.read()
    # LM35 gives 10mV per degree Celsius, conversion assuming 3.3V
reference voltage and 12-bit ADC (0-4095)
    temperature = (adc_value / 4095.0) * 3.3 * 100  # Example
conversion for LM35 (in degrees Celsius)

    # HTML page to display temperature
    html = """<html>
    <head><title>ESP32 Temperature Monitor</title></head>
    <body>
    <p>Current Temperature: <strong>{:.2f} °C</strong></p>
    </body></html>""".format(temperature)
    return html

# Handle incoming HTTP requests
while True:
    conn, addr = server.accept()  # Accept connection from client
    print("Client connected from:", addr)
    request = conn.recv(1024).decode()  # Get the request
    print("Request:", request)

    # Send the response (temperature reading in HTML)
    response = web_page()
    conn.send("HTTP/1.1 200 OK\n")
    conn.send("Content-Type: text/html\n\n")
    conn.sendall(response)
    conn.close()  # Close the connection
```

Upload the Code to ESP32:

- *Use an IDE like Thonny or another MicroPython-compatible tool.*
- *Connect the ESP32 to your computer via USB and configure Thonny for ESP32.*
- *Copy and paste the code into the IDE.*
- *Save the file as main.py on your ESP32.*
- *Click "Run" to execute the code.*

Check Output:

- *Once the ESP32 connects to Wi-Fi, it will print the IP address in the console (e.g., Connected to Wi-Fi with IP: 192.168.1.x).*
- *Open a web browser and enter the IP address displayed in the console.*
- *The browser will load a simple webpage showing the current temperature in degrees Celsius.*

← → C ⚠ Not secure 192.168.1.107/

Current Temperature: **0.64 °C**

Note
- Replace "YourNetworkSSID" and "YourNetworkPassword" with your Wi-Fi credentials to connect successfully.
- The printed IP address after connection will be used to access the temperature monitoring page in a web browser, e.g., http://192.168.1.50.
- The conversion of the ADC value depends on the sensor you use. The example provided is for an LM35 sensor, which outputs a voltage that directly corresponds to temperature (in degrees Celsius). Adjust the conversion if using a different sensor.

4. Request Data Retrieval Functions
Understanding arg(), uri(), method(), and hasArg() Functions in MicroPython for ESP32/ESP8266

What is
arg(), uri(), method(), and hasArg() are functions used to manage and interact with HTTP requests when working with ESP32 or ESP8266 using MicroPython. They are used to handle incoming request parameters, retrieve specific request information, and determine which HTTP methods are in use.

Why is Important?
These functions are essential for controlling HTTP communication when using ESP32/ESP8266 as a web server or client. They help in parsing requests and creating interactive IoT applications, making your ESP8266 or ESP32-based devices smarter and more functional.

Syntax

```
arg(argument_name)
uri()
method()
hasArg(argument_name)
```

Syntax Explanation

- *arg(argument_name)*: Retrieves the value of the specified argument in the HTTP request.
- *uri()*: Returns the URI (Uniform Resource Identifier) of the incoming HTTP request.
- *method()*: Indicates the type of HTTP method used in the request (e.g., GET or POST).
- *hasArg(argument_name)*: Checks if a specific argument is present in the HTTP request and returns a boolean value (True or False).

Code Example

```
if server.hasArg('temperature'):
    temperature_value = server.arg('temperature')
    print('Temperature: ', temperature_value)
```

Notes

- These functions are commonly used when you want to build a web interface that allows users to interact with your ESP32/ESP8266 device, for example, to submit data via forms.
- Ensure that your ESP device is properly connected to the local network to use these features effectively.

Warnings

- The functions should be used within an appropriate HTTP server framework for ESP32/ESP8266 in MicroPython, otherwise, they won't work properly.
- Improper parsing of arguments may lead to potential security vulnerabilities like injection attacks if inputs are not sanitized properly.

Project Title: Wi-Fi Network Configurator for ESP32 and ESP8266

Objective
To create a simple and easy-to-use Wi-Fi Network Configurator using MicroPython for ESP32 and ESP8266, allowing users to connect the device to a specified Wi-Fi network through a web interface.

Programming Fundamentals
- *import*: Used to include necessary libraries, such as *network* and *socket*, that provide network control capabilities.
- *class*: Defines the structure of the project by grouping related functions and data together for reusability and organization.
- *def*: Defines functions that carry out specific tasks, like connecting to Wi-Fi or handling HTTP requests.
- *while*: Implements a loop for repeatedly checking connection status or continuously running the server.
- *try/except*: Helps in handling errors like incorrect Wi-Fi credentials or connection failures, providing a stable user experience.

Use Syntax
```
import network
import socket
station = network.WLAN(network.STA_IF)
station.connect('SSID', 'password')
if station.isconnected():
server_socket = socket.socket(socket.AF_INET, socket.SOCK_STREAM)
```

Requirement Component
1. ESP32 or ESP8266 board
2. Micro USB cable
3. Computer with USB port for flashing MicroPython
4. Breadboard (optional, for easier connections)
5. Jumper wires (optional)

Circuit Diagram
- Not necessary for this project, as it primarily involves configuring Wi-Fi settings on the board.
- If needed, you can connect an LED to GPIO for visual indication of Wi-Fi status.

Circuit Connection

1. Connect the ESP32 or ESP8266 to the computer via a USB cable for power and programming.
2. Optionally, connect an LED to GPIO pin 2 and GND to indicate Wi-Fi connection status.

MicroPython Code

```python
import network
import socket
import time

# Replace with your Wi-Fi credentials
ssid = 'your_SSID'
password = 'your_password'

# Set up the Wi-Fi connection
station = network.WLAN(network.STA_IF)
station.active(True)
station.connect(ssid, password)

# Wait until connected to Wi-Fi
while not station.isconnected():
    time.sleep(1)

print('Connected, IP Address:', station.ifconfig()[0])

# Set up the server socket
server_socket = socket.socket(socket.AF_INET, socket.SOCK_STREAM)
server_socket.bind(('', 80))  # Bind to port 80 (HTTP port)
server_socket.listen(5)  # Listen for incoming connections

# Main loop to handle client connections
while True:
    # Accept connection from client
    client, addr = server_socket.accept()
    print('Client connected from', addr)

    # Receive the client request
    request = client.recv(1024)
    print('Request:', request)

    # Send the HTTP response
    response = """HTTP/1.1 200 OK\r\nContent-Type: text/html\r\n\r\n
    <html><body><h1>Wi-Fi Configurator</h1></body></html>"""
    client.send(response.encode())

    # Close the client connection
    client.close()
```

Upload the Code to ESP32:
- Use an IDE like Thonny or another MicroPython-compatible tool.
- Connect the ESP32 to your computer via USB and configure Thonny for ESP32.
- Copy the above code and paste it into Thonny.
- Save the file as `main.py` on your ESP32.
- Click "Run" to execute the code.

Check the Output:
- Once the code runs, it will connect the ESP32 to the specified Wi-Fi network.
- The console will display the message `Connected, IP Address:` followed by the IP address of the ESP32.
- Open a web browser on any device connected to the same network and enter the IP address of the ESP32.
- You should see a web page displaying "Wi-Fi Configurator".

Note
- Make sure to replace *'your_SSID'* and *'your_password'* with your actual Wi-Fi credentials.
- The provided example is a simple configurator that can be extended to include a web form for entering SSID and password dynamically.
- If the ESP board doesn't connect, ensure your Wi-Fi credentials are correct, and that the router is within range.

Understanding *arg()* and *hasArg()* Functions in MicroPython for ESP32/ESP8266

What is
arg() and *hasArg()* are functions used in MicroPython for handling HTTP requests when working with ESP32 or ESP8266 devices. These functions allow you to extract and check for parameters within incoming requests, making it easier to interact with data received through a web server.

Why is Important
These functions are crucial for building interactive web servers on ESP32/ESP8266 devices, as they allow you to extract user input

from the URL or forms. This interaction makes it possible to control hardware, set configurations, or collect data, enabling the ESP device to become more versatile.

Syntax

```
arg(argument_name)
hasArg(argument_name)
```

Syntax Explanation

- *arg(argument_name)*: Retrieves the value of a specified argument in the incoming HTTP request, where *argument_name* is the name of the parameter you want to extract.
- *hasArg(argument_name)*: Checks if a specific argument is present in the HTTP request, returning *True* if found, otherwise *False*.

Code Example

```
if server.hasArg('led'):
    led_state = server.arg('led')
    print('LED state: ', led_state)
```

Notes

- *arg()* and *hasArg()* are usually used together to safely extract arguments from an incoming request after verifying that the parameter exists.
- They are generally used when setting up a basic web server on ESP32/ESP8266, allowing the user to pass commands via URL parameters.

Warnings

- Always validate input received through *arg()* to prevent potential security vulnerabilities such as code injection or unexpected input behavior.
- Ensure your ESP device has an active network connection to receive requests and make use of these functions effectively.

Project : IoT Control with Parameters: LED Brightness Control Using Browser Input

Objective
To create an IoT project using MicroPython on ESP32 or ESP8266 that allows controlling the brightness of an LED by adjusting a parameter sent from a web browser.

Programming Fundamentals
- *import*: Used to include necessary modules, such as *machine*, *network*, and *socket*, which help control hardware pins, network connections, and HTTP communication.
- *class*: Organizes code into reusable and logical structures, making it easier to manage the web server and hardware interactions.
- *def*: Defines reusable functions to handle tasks like connecting to Wi-Fi, setting up a web server, and controlling LED brightness.
- *while*: Implements a loop for continuously running the web server, enabling real-time interaction.
- *try/except*: Handles errors, such as unexpected input values, preventing the program from crashing.

Use Syntax

```
import machine import network import socket pwm =
machine.PWM(machine.Pin(2), freq=1000)
pwm.duty(int(brightness))
```

Requirement Component
1. ESP32 or ESP8266 board
2. Micro USB cable
3. Computer for programming and power
4. LED
5. Resistor (220 ohms)
6. Breadboard and jumper wires

Circuit Diagram
1. Connect the positive leg of the LED to GPIO 2 on the ESP32 or ESP8266.
2. Connect the negative leg of the LED to the resistor, and connect the other side of the resistor to GND.

Circuit Connection
1. ESP32/ESP8266 GPIO 2 -> LED positive leg (anode).
2. LED negative leg (cathode) -> Resistor (220 ohms) -> GND of ESP32/ESP8266.
3. Connect the ESP board to the computer using a USB cable.

MicroPython Code

```python
import machine
import network
import socket

# Replace with your Wi-Fi credentials
ssid = 'your_SSID'
password = 'your_password'

# Set up the Wi-Fi connection
station = network.WLAN(network.STA_IF)
station.active(True)
station.connect(ssid, password)

# Wait until connected to Wi-Fi
while not station.isconnected():
    pass

print('Connected, IP Address:', station.ifconfig()[0])

# Set up PWM on GPIO 2 (can be connected to an LED)
pwm = machine.PWM(machine.Pin(2), freq=1000)

# Set up the web server
server_socket = socket.socket(socket.AF_INET, socket.SOCK_STREAM)
server_socket.bind(('', 80))  # Bind to port 80 (HTTP)
server_socket.listen(5)  # Listen for incoming connections

# Main loop to handle client connections
while True:
    client, addr = server_socket.accept()  # Accept connection from
client
    print('Client connected from', addr)

    # Receive the client request
    request = client.recv(1024).decode('utf-8')
    print('Request:', request)

    # Check if a brightness value is provided
    if 'GET /?brightness=' in request:
        brightness_value = request.split('/?brightness=')[1].split('
')[0]
        try:
            brightness = int(brightness_value)  # Convert to integer
            if 0 <= brightness <= 1023:  # Ensure brightness is within
the valid range
                pwm.duty(brightness)  # Set the PWM duty cycle (0-1023)
            else:
```

```
        print('Brightness value out of range (0-1023)')
    except ValueError:
        print('Invalid brightness value')

# Send the HTTP response with the HTML form
response = """HTTP/1.1 200 OK\r\nContent-Type: text/html\r\n\r\n
<html><body><h1>LED Brightness Control</h1>
<form action="/" method="get">
Brightness (0-1023): <input type="number" name="brightness">
<input type="submit" value="Set">
</form></body></html>"""
client.send(response.encode())

# Close the client connection
client.close()
```

Upload the Code to ESP32:

Use an IDE like Thonny or another MicroPython-compatible tool.
Connect the ESP32 to your computer via USB and configure
Thonny for ESP32.
Copy and paste the code into the IDE.
Save the file as main.py on your ESP32.
Click "Run" to execute the code.

Check the Output:

Once the ESP32 connects to the Wi-Fi, it will display the IP address
in the console.
Open a web browser and enter the ESP32's IP address (e.g.,
http://192.168.1.x).
You will see a web page with a form to input the brightness value.
Enter a number between 0 and 1023 and click "Set" to adjust the
LED's brightness.

Note
- Make sure to replace *'your_SSID'* and *'your_password'* with
  the actual Wi-Fi credentials.
- The brightness value must be between *0* and *1023*, where *0*
  turns the LED off and *1023* sets it to full brightness.
- This example uses PWM to vary the LED's brightness, and
  the browser interface allows real-time interaction with the
  hardware.

www.ingramcontent.com/pod-product-compliance
Lightning Source LLC
La Vergne TN
LVHW051330050326
832903LV00031B/3467